Speaker's Meaning

Owen Barfield

Speaker's Meaning

WESLEYAN UNIVERSITY PRESS
Middletown, Connecticut

All inquiries and permissions requests should be addressed to the Publisher, Wesleyan University Press, 110 Mt. Vernon Street, Middletown, Connecticut 06457.

Library of Congress Card Number: 67–24113
ISBN: 0–8195–6113–4

Manufactured in the United States of America

Wesleyan Paperback, 1984

93   92   91   90   89   6   5   4   3   2

Contents

Foreword

1   The Semantic Approach to History
and the Historical Approach
to the Study of Meaning   13

2   Imagery in Language and
Metaphor in Poetry   40

3   The Psychology of Inspiration
and of Imagination   68

4   Subject and Object in the
History of Meaning   92

FEW AND UNIMPORTANT would the errors of men be, if they did but know, first what they themselves mean: and secondly, what the *words* mean by which they attempt to convey their meaning.

— S. T. COLERIDGE

(*Letter to Thomas Allsop;* December 2, 1818)

Foreword

WHAT FOLLOWS REPRODUCES, with some alterations and additions, four public lectures which I was invited to deliver in the fall of 1965 during a year's teaching in the Department of English and American Literature of Brandeis University, Waltham, Massachusetts. They were conceived and born in response to that invitation. The small but increasing number of British subjects who have themselves experienced the warm atmosphere of hospitality and personal welcome with which the faculty and students of an American university are wont to surround a Visiting Professor from the day of his arrival to the day of his departure will be able to guess how very much more I owe to the community of Brandeis than the accident of their having been the only begetters of this little book.

Speaker's Meaning

CHAPTER I

The Semantic Approach to History
and the Historical Approach
to the Study of Meaning

IT IS PERHAPS not as widely appreciated as it might be that real interest in history is a comparatively recent phenomenon. If we mean by "history" something involving an imaginative concern with the past, some sort of reconstruction of the past in the imagination of the present, then, in spite of Herodotus, Thucydides, and Tacitus, we must admit that the Greeks and Romans and their predecessors were just not interested in the past in that way. The same is true of their successors down to about the seventeenth century A.D.

Certainly they were interested in persons no longer living and in past events, but only for reasons of family or national prestige or as paradigms of human nature and human behaviour in general. Renaissance humanism did indeed possess, as Erich Auerbach insisted in the chapter of *Mimesis* which he devoted to Shakespeare, a historical "perspective." It contrasted antiquity with the present age; but its interest in antiquity as a whole was also paradigmatic. Classical civilization was a model which it not only admired but was anxious, if possible, to restore. This is quite different from that concern with the past for its own sake with which a century and a half of historical novels has made *us* familiar. It is different from an interest in the past *as* past—the kind of interest that would have made it impossible for Shakespeare to put into the mouth of Theseus (anticipating the invention of gunpowder in the West by some 2,000 years or so) his graphic description of

> — russet-pated choughs, many in sort,
> Rising and cawing at the gun's report.

Logan Pearsall Smith once drew attention to the fact that the word "anachronism" was first used in its present sense (appropriate to *this* age, but out of joint with *that*) by Coleridge, that even the distinction between *ancient* and *modern* first appears in Bacon's writings and that the word "prehistoric" is not found at all before 1856. After quoting a large number of similar instances, he summarized as follows:

> If we examine our historical vocabulary, the words and phrases by which we express our sense that the past was not the same, but something different from the present, we shall find that they are all of them modern and most of them indeed of very recent introduction.[1]

But this sense of the past as "something different" is almost inseparable from another element in our own concern with history, namely, the habit of looking on the past as a sort of seed, of which the present is the transformation or fruit. This "developmental" view of the nature of time past seems to us so obvious as to make it almost nonsensical to put it into words; for whether we think of history in general as a meaningful process or as a meaningless one, we just cannot help thinking of it as the old gradually giving way to the new. Yet that whole way of thinking is hardly more than two or three centuries old. It began only when another

1. Logan Pearsall Smith, *The English Language*, Ch. ix. London, Williams & Norgate, Ltd. (Home University Library), 1918; New York, Henry Holt & Co., 1912.

important change had just been taking place in the West in men's ideas about the relation between past and present. This change, of which an admirably detailed account was given by J. B. Bury in *The Idea of Progress*,[2] was the abandonment of the medieval and classical conviction that the history of mankind as whole was a process of degeneration, and the substitution therefor of the conviction that the history of man is one of progress. Hitherto it had been thought of as a *descent* from a Golden Age in the past; now it began to be thought of as an *ascent* into a golden age in the future.

It would be possible to trace the various modifications this new approach to history has undergone since its first appearance: the notion, for instance, (as old as Vico and as young as Spengler) of history as a series of cycles; then the tendency to treat these cycles as organisms, with their own rhythm of growth, maturity, and decay; and so on. But, leaving all that aside, let us rather ask what it is that most strikingly characterizes the subject of history as it stands today.

Professor Toynbee called his monumental

2. John B. Bury, *The Idea of Progress*. London, Macmillan & Co., Ltd., 1920; New York, The Macmillan Company, 1932.

work not a history or an "outline of history," but a "study" of history. That is, not only a history, but a theory of the *nature* of history. And indeed, today there is as much interest in historiography as in history itself. No one is quite sure what history actually is or even if there is such a thing. At the same time there is a passionate interest in it. I say, "or even if there is such a thing," because there is, of course, a flourishing antihistorical school, which denies any persistent coherence to the long-term order of events and maintains, in effect, with Henry Ford, that "history is bunk."

It was in this respect that R. G. Collingwood, in the introductory section to his book *The Idea of History*,[3] compared our attitude today toward this relatively new subject with the attitude that prevailed in the seventeenth century to the then new subject of natural science. There is, he said, the same uncertainty, the same excitement; the same rashness in sweeping generalizations; the same excessive caution on one side contrasted with the same over-exuberant claims made by the other.

Notice however that it was only in this re-

3. R. G. Collingwood, *The Idea of History*. Oxford, Clarendon Press, 1946; New York, Oxford Paperbacks, 1961.

spect that Collingwood likened history to natural science. In other respects he contrasted them very sharply indeed; and it will be my first task to look a little further into both the resemblance and the difference between the two disciplines, which this philosopher of history divined.

Natural science was originally called "natural philosophy," and one may say that the excitement and uncertainty which prevailed in the seventeenth century accompanied the slowly dawning realization that natural science (or science as we now generally call it) could no longer continue to be treated as a species or subclass of philosophy, but had acquired a separate existence of its own; that it amounted to an entirely new method of cognition—a new way of approaching experience as a whole. And since it was a new way of approaching experience as a whole, it soon came to be inferred that the new method must be applied, not only to the investigation of natural phenomena, but in every conceivable field of inquiry, including the one we call history. Throughout the nineteenth century, it was assumed that the scientific method was the only reliable way in which history could be tackled.

This last inference, says Collingwood, was a

mistake. Just as science began life as a department of philosophy and then emerged into a separate existence in its own right, so history itself is today emerging from the position it has too long occupied as a subdepartment of science into a separate existence as a parallel and autonomous method of cognition, as a valid approach to experience as a whole.

The basis on which he draws his sharp dividing line between history and science is the fact that the historian's actual raw material is never *events* themselves, but always one or more *records* of events. Whereas the events themselves, if they could be investigated while they were actually occurring, might perhaps be treated scientifically, this is simply not possible with the written records, which are in fact all that the historian has before him. For these records were produced by individuals, and by individuals with all sorts of mental preoccupations; in the case of ancient records, they were produced by human beings with an entirely different "mental set" from our own. Moreover a record, even if it is made later on by someone who had actually participated in the event recorded (which is very rarely the case), always represents or reproduces, not the event itself, but the writer's memory of the event—a very different matter.

So far away are the data of the historian from the data with which natural science has to deal, and can properly deal, by its own methods! But that is not all. History is not even the past recorded. Records, however numerous and exact, are still not themselves history. They are only the raw material of history. History itself only comes into being when that which was recorded is brought to life—realized—in the mind of the historian. Thus history, according to Collingwood, is the past "re-enacted" in the mind of the historian and his reader. Anything less than this is not history but a bare chronicle, a calendar, a string of dates. This reflection leads him to his well-known, and audacious, conclusion that "all real history is history of thought."

Briefly, then, his argument is that history is only possible at all to the extent that the past is still living on in the present—living on as what he calls "the self-conscious historical life" of the historian and his reader. It is when we go on to ask him what exactly he means by this "self-conscious historical life" that we come to the real basis of his sharp distinction between history and science. For his reply is that historical events are distinguished from natural events (which are the raw material of science) by the fact that they have both an "inside" and an "outside." The "inside" of a historical event is "that in it which can only be described in terms of thought." He exemplifies in this way:

> By the outside of an event I mean everything belonging to it which can be described in terms of bodies and their movements: the passage of Caesar, accompanied by certain men, across a certain river called the Rubicon at one date, or the spilling of his blood on the floor of the senate-house at another. By the inside of an event I mean that in it which can only be described in terms of thought: Caesar's defiance of Republican law, or the clash of constitutional policy between himself and his assassins.

History is possible precisely because the historian can re-enact in his own mind the "inside" of a past event, the thought content which it includes.

Here, without pausing to examine this view of history in detail or to state in what respects I myself accept it and in what respects I do not, I stress that it is founded on a certain very definite conviction; namely, that there is a sense in which the past is living on—or can be made to live on—in the present. And I do so because I believe that it is this *way* of looking back, or trying to look back, into the past arising from just this conviction (whether explicit, as in Collingwood's case, or more implicitly) that most strikingly characterizes our approach to history today.

There were, of course, older ways of feeling that the past is still effective in the present, ways connected not so much with the free and voluntary activity of thought as with the bloodstream: as, for instance, when the generality of Western mankind could still feel that they themselves, and all men living in their own time, were guilty of the sin committed by their physical ancestor, Adam. But this other and newer sense, the sense of a *stored* past, a past accessible to detailed research and yet also (and for that reason) alive and effective in the present, is quite different. For here the past is conceived to be alive and effective, rather as *memory* is alive and effective, in the "self-consciousness" of the present. I have mentioned only Collingwood, but I suggest that this more living relation in thought to the past is the one to which historical study in general (I exclude, of course, the antihistorical school) is on the whole more and more tending.

Nevertheless, when Collingwood speaks of the historian "re-enacting" the thought of Caesar as he crossed the Rubicon—still more when he insists (as he does) that the thought in Caesar's mind and the thought in the mind of the historian of Caesar are "not two thoughts but one and the same thought," some of his critics grow uneasy. What on earth does he mean by this "re-enacting"? How can two thoughts be one and the same thought? And with these two unanswered questions, I propose to turn aside from Collingwood and his *Idea of History* and return to them later. I think it more helpful at this juncture to reflect on the fact that, however it may be with historical study, there is one case where the past certainly does live on in the present, as the thought of the present, and as the self-consciousness of the present; one case where we certainly do re-enact—and really there can hardly be a better way of putting it—in the present the thinking of the past . . . although we are not often very keenly aware that that is what we are doing. Is it not exactly what we do whenever we speak or write? When we use a word, we re-enact, or adopt, or reanimate, or entertain the thought of previous users of the same word or some part at least of that thought. It may be a very small part indeed. But we must be doing just that thing to some extent; for otherwise we should not be uttering a word at all, but simply making a noise! Of course the same thing is true of the previous speakers themselves, and of other speakers before them—until you get back to the first occasion on which that word was used, or to the veiled and problematic origin of language itself.

Now, without going back as far as that, it is in fact often possible to trace well into the past the way, or ways, in which previous speakers and writers have used many of the words we are still using today. Thus, if you take some common word in constant use ("idea," for instance, or "species," "cause," "general," "matter," "form," or "nature") you find that in order to discover as a matter of history how it came to be used as it is today, you must traverse many centuries. In the case of "idea," you must go back at least as far as Plato, and even into the impact of Aristotelian upon Platonic thought and somewhat also into the whole subsequent history of philosophy and of Western thought in general. You will also have to take into account the transferences of thought, or meaning, from one language into another—such as occurred when the word "species" was used to translate the Aristotelian "idea" or *eidos*. To study in this way the thought previously expressed from time to time by words in daily use is to make what I would call the semantic approach to history. But it is also, and at the same time, to make the historical approach to semantics; for another way of putting it would be to say that what we are studying is the way in which these words have come to mean what they do mean. In either case I am persuaded that this approach is a very useful supplementary one to any other we care to make.

My own slight attempt at a semantic approach to Western history is to be found in *History in English Words*.[4] Although many other far more learned studies have been made of various words and their histories, I do not myself know of any other attempt so far to apply the method systematically (or at least semisystematically) to the study of history in general—to use it in fact as a means rather than

4. Owen Barfield, *History in English Words*. London, Faber & Faber Ltd., 1954; Grand Rapids, Michigan, Wm. B. Eerdmans Publishing Co., 1966.

an end in itself. It was an elementary attempt, on popular lines, and the task could with advantage be performed at much greater length and much better by better scholars. Even so, it will suffice to show that the half-dozen words I have mentioned are merely random examples taken from a host whose name is legion.

I hope these may suffice by themselves to illustrate the sort of thing I mean; for my purpose now is not to make the approach all over again, but to speak of the theory underlying such an approach. In that connection the question naturally arises, Am I suggesting that every time a common word (let us say, the word "nature") is used by someone today, all the thought—or all the thought and feeling—which all previous users ever employed it to express is somehow re-enacted or entertained by the current speaker? Of course the answer is no! I said we adopt or entertain the thought of previous users of the word "or some part of it" and I added that it might be a very small part indeed.

It may be noticeable that I have made comparatively little use, so far, of the word "meaning"; although any ordinary person would say that that has been my topic throughout the last few paragraphs. Meaning is of course a very undefinable (and in our time a highly controversial) term. So let us put it a little more precisely and say that my topic has been the "dictionary meanings" of words, or (because it is a little shorter) their "lexical" meanings. We shall not get much further unless we appreciate that from this we have to distinguish what I will call the "speaker's meaning." C. S. Lewis, in his *Studies in Words*,[5] gives a very striking example of the difference between this lexical meaning, which he also sometimes calls the "word's force," on the one hand, and the speaker's intention, on the other hand. The lexical meaning of the word "supper" is, approximately, "a supernumerary meal which, if taken at all, is the last meal before bed," but "when I spoke of supper after the theatre, I meant by supper a biscuit and a cup of cocoa. But my friend meant by supper something like a cold bird and a bottle of wine." It may be assumed nevertheless that both "I" and "my friend" were equally well aware of the lexical meaning.

Here you have a simple example of how the

5. C. S. Lewis, *Studies in Words*. London and New York, Cambridge University Press, 1960.

difference between the lexical meaning and a particular speaker's meaning (even in ordinary humdrum human intercourse) may become a source of agonizing confusion, and even perhaps contention. Why? Because it has been the cause of imperfect communication. How much more will that be so in the case of words much less easy to define than "supper."

Now it is upon this all-important distinction between the speaker's intention and the "word's force," or between the speaker's meaning and the lexical meaning (regarded as a source of imperfect communication), that linguistic analysis has exercised most of its agility. One could say that, in so far as linguistic analysis has a "purpose" or "aim," its aim is to eliminate that discrepancy wherever possible and thus to bring about a more accurate communication between human minds (or perhaps it would be safer to say between human organisms). As a help toward this, we ought to be very careful how we talk about words "having" meanings at all. Words do not contain meanings as a cigarette box contains cigarettes; and linguistic analysis points out that the so-called meaning of a word or sentence is simply the way in which it is used, or that language means what it is normally used to mean. That is a healthy reminder. We may perhaps feel that some linguistic philosophers overestimate the simple-mindedness of the rest of us in these matters; but their basic approach is helpful. The actual meaning of a word must be regarded as a kind of habit, the normal habit of contemporary people when they speak or write; and a good dictionary will contain the best way possible of recording or describing that habit. The lexical meaning of a word is a kind of norm.

But of course that does not dispose of all our difficulties; no good analyst would maintain that it does. One difficulty, of which I myself am very aware, is that of determining what is to be considered a "wrong" or "mistaken" use of language. Of course the criterion may be simple enough in any particular case. A wrong use of language must be any departure from the norm. If today, for example, I used the word "officious" in the way it was used two hundred years ago, intending to imply helpfulness or charity,[6] I should be using it wrongly. The difficulty arises when the mistaken use is said to be wide-

6. As in Johnson's poem on the death of his friend Levitt: "Officious, innocent, sincere. See Levitt to the grave descend!"

spread, or even universal—because (by definition) the most widespread use of language constitutes the norm and is therefore its "right" meaning. Can everybody make the same linguistic mistakes? Or, can any group of speakers of the same language make the same mistakes and go on making them from generation to generation? My own answer here would be no. From the criterion of "normal usage" it must follow that whatever illusions our ancestors may all have shared, these illusions cannot have arisen from a mistaken use of language. The question might even seem an unnecessary one, if it were not for the fact that a mistaken use of language is just what linguistic analysis appears to maintain that almost everybody has been making almost all the time.

Possibly there is some analytical answer to this puzzle; indeed I think I have encountered some attempts at them, but I have never found any that satisfied. However, all I really want to suggest now is that the lexical meanings of words (that is, the ways in which they are being used at any given time) is clearly such an intricate and subtle matter that it needs, for full comprehension, a historical approach to supplement the analytical or empirical one. It is a historical fact that those elusive norms we loosely call "meanings" are involved in a constant process of change. It would moreover not be very difficult to demonstrate that all mental progress (and, arising from that, all material progress) is brought about in association with those very changes. One can go further and say that the changes are made possible precisely by that discrepancy between an individual speaker's meaning and the current, or lexical, meaning.

"If some speaker's meaning," says Lewis in the book already referred to, "becomes very common, it will in the end establish itself as one of the word's meanings; this is one of the ways in which semantic ramification comes about." He goes on to take the simple example of the word "furniture":

> For thousands of Englishmen today the word *furniture* has only one sense—a (not very easily definable) class of domestic movables. And doubtless many people, if they should read Berkeley's 'all the choir of heaven and furniture of earth', would take this use of *furniture* to be a metaphorical application of the sense they know—that which is to earth as tables and chairs and so forth are to a house. Even those who know

the larger meaning of the word (whatever 'furnishes' in the sense of stocking, equipping or replenishing) would certainly admit 'domestic movables' as one of its senses. . . . But it must have become one of the word's meanings by becoming a very common speaker's meaning. Men who said 'my furniture' were often in fact, within that context, referring to their domestic movables. The word did not yet mean that; *they* meant it. When I say 'Take away this rubbish' I usually 'mean' these piles of old newspapers, magazines, and Christmas cards. That is not what the word *rubbish* means. But if a sufficiently large number of people shared my distaste for that sort of litter, and applied the word *rubbish* to it often enough, the word might come to have this as one of its senses. So with *furniture*, which, from being a speaker's meaning, has established itself so firmly as one of the word's meanings that it has ousted all the others in popular speech.

There you have an example of the speaker's meaning interacting with the lexical meaning in a way that results in a certain contraction. It is however more the other kind of interaction—the kind that brings about an *expansion* of meaning (or a wider extension of the term), with which, as we shall see, our mental and material progress is especially associated.

At the moment the point is that, one way or another (for there are other types of meaning-change besides expansion and contraction), *the norms themselves are continually changing.* Somehow what was normal yesterday becomes abnormal today, and vice versa. Moreover the changes are sometimes so radical as to be enormous. They can even amount to a *volte face.* One example of this (which involves a glance forward to Chapter 4) would be the word "subjective." Originally it was used to signify "existing or being in itself, or independently." It was the existential predicate par excellence. Today it is used to denote the exact opposite: "existing, if at all, *only* in someone's mind." Moreover many common words cannot be said to have achieved a single semantic norm at all. An all too obvious example is the vocabulary of sociology and politics—words like "democracy," "freedom," "peace-loving," "bourgeois." But, quite apart from this special case (where there are axes to grind), ordinary educated language is full of such words. Thus, "natural" is sometimes used as if it meant "the opposite of human"; at other times "the opposite of artificial" and at other times again, "organic as distinct from inorganic"; at others yet again, "good rather than evil" or (in the theology of grace) "evil rather than good." Finally there are not a few who would say that the word "nature" really signifies "all that is or happens, the whole show, the universe"—or just "everything"! Each of these conflicting norms has a traceable history of its own.

It does seem that if we are interested in the meanings of words or in their normal usage *at all*, then, unless we are very incurious indeed, we shall want to know something of how these meanings were arrived at. We shall find something to interest us, for example, in the fifty pages of C. S. Lewis's *Studies in Words*, which he actually devotes to all these different ways of using the word "nature," and in which he traces, with care and erudition, the various ways in which a speaker's meaning and a lexical meaning have interacted from time to time to bring about the present state of affairs.

To sum up: the single phenomenon of the difference between these two aspects of meaning (lexical and speaker's) is of importance to us in two very different ways: first, because it is an important key to the history of the human mind and human civilization; second, because it is a source of imperfect communication between human beings. It may seem odd perhaps that it should contrive to be both these things at one and the same time. Indeed it may sometimes appear that the study of language and of the nature of language from the semantic point of view is an impenetrable jungle. If so, we must either give up the study altogether or else we must try (to begin with) to cut at least one broad path through the jungle, by which we can then conduct our further operations. Here is one such path which I myself have found particularly useful, though it is not by any means the only possible starting point.

Language has two primary functions, one of which is expression and the other communication. They are not the only functions language performs, but they are both indispensable to its existence. The goal to which expression aspires, or the criterion by which it must be measured, is something like fullness or sincerity. The goal toward which communication aspires is accuracy. Both functions must be performed *in some degree*—and at the same time—otherwise there is no language at all. But the extent to which either function predominates over the other will vary greatly. To exemplify by extreme instances: when language is properly used to define the position of a ship at sea, you have a maximum of communication and a minimum of expression; and for that reason the communication can be very nearly perfect. It can achieve total accuracy. (It could of course be argued that things like that can be done even better without using language at all, by mathematics. But I see no objection to regarding mathematics as the *terminus ad quem* of a language aiming at perfect accuracy to the exclusion of all else. All that is in the domain of information theory.)

At the opposite extreme a maximum of expression, with a minimum of communication, would occur in the case, let us say, of a poet, with a genuinely rich psyche, wide powers of observation, great emotional depth, etc., but who was nevertheless, unfortunately, a *bad* poet—so that few, if any, of his readers were led to share that observation and that emotion.

Here we get a glimpse of the true relation between the two functions. On the one hand they tend to be mutually exclusive; so that Expression could say to Communication, in the words of Alice's Duchess, "The more there is of mine, the less there is of yours"; but on the other hand the relation is a *dynamic* rather than a *quantitative* one. This means that, though each of them is exclusive of, or counter to, the other, yet they are both concurrently necessary. They are, so to speak, "sweet enemies." There is a tension, or polarity, between them. And it is in this polarity that the depths of language are to be found. The two functions conflict, but they also co-operate. You can say, if you like, that the concern of communication is with the *how*, whereas the concern of expression is with the *what*. Perfect communication would occur if all words had and retained identical meanings every time they were uttered and heard. But it would occur at the expense of expression. In the same way, perfect individual or personal expression can only be achieved at the expense of communication, or at all events, at the expense of accuracy in communication. It is not much use having a perfect means of communication if you have nothing to communicate except the relative positions of bodies in space—or if you will never again have anything *new* to communicate. In the same way it is not much use expressing yourself very fully and perfectly indeed—if nobody can understand a word you are saying.

I hope all this may have emphasised not simply the rather trite and obvious point that the instrument of language performs the double function of communication and expression,[7] but the peculiar nature of the *relation between* those two functions—the relation, namely, of a polarity of contraries. A polarity of contraries is not quite the same as the *coincidentia oppositorum,* which has been stressed by some philosophers, or as the "paradox" which (whether for the purposes of irony or for other reasons) is beloved by some contemporary writers and critics. A paradox is the violent union of two opposites that simply contradict each other, so that reason assures us we can have one *or* the other but not both at the same time. Whereas polar contraries (as is illustrated by the use of the term in electricity) exist by virtue of each other *as well as* at each other's expense. For that very reason the concept of polarity cannot be subsumed under

7. As Mr. Noam Chomsky has recently reminded us in *Cartesian Linguistics* (New York, Harper & Row, Publishers, Inc., 1966), recognition of the two functions is at least as old as the seventeenth century, besides being as modern as "generative grammar." It appears in fact to be indispensable to any handling of language that does not willfully shut its eyes to the fact and the problem of expansion of meaning.

the logical principle of identity; in fact, it is not really a logical concept at all, but one which requires an act of imagination to grasp it. Coleridge applied to it such terms as "projective unity" and "separative projection." Unlike the logical principles of identity and contradiction, it is not only a form of thought, but also the form of life. It could perhaps be called the principle of seminal identity. It is also the formal principle which underlies meaning itself and the expansion of meaning.

CHAPTER 2

Imagery in Language
and Metaphor in Poetry

ONE OF THE POINTS I MADE, and indeed insisted on, in the previous chapter was that if we are really convinced that the so-called meaning of language is simply the way in which it is normally used by normal people, then, short of putting on blinkers, we cannot avoid seeing that the meanings of a great many words change as time goes on. There are moreover certain characteristic changes, one of which is contraction. The meaning of the word, or the extension of the term, shrinks, so that it comes to denote (as has happened with the word "furniture") only one particular part of some larger area or category, the whole of which it formerly included.

Of course this is not the only way in which the meanings of words change in course of time.

There is also the opposite way, which may be called expansion. Somehow or other a word or a phrase begins to mean *more* or much more than it has meant hitherto. An interesting example of this would be "gravity" and its more recent companion "gravitation." Down to the seventeenth or eighteenth century "gravity" in its physical sense (we can omit the psychological one) was virtually a synonym for heaviness or weight—the quality which leads solid objects to seek the center of the earth. Whereas, since Newton's time, both words have come to mean, when normally used by normal people, a force or law operative not only in the sublunary sphere, but throughout the wide spaces of the universe. Another example would be the word "focus," a Latin word adopted into English, and a term mainly used in optics and geometry. In classical Latin "focus" was the word for hearth—and in particular the fire burning on the hearth. It continued to have the same restricted meaning in medieval Latin, until the astronomer Kepler (writing in Latin) made use of it for his own purposes. With its adoption into English the earlier meaning was dropped altogether.

Both these examples, as is appropriate in a

scientific age, are taken from the progress of science. That is in the context accidental, but it makes them particularly useful examples, because here we know what was going on and can therefore actually observe the impact of the speaker's meaning on lexical meaning which brought about the change. It is not often as clear or as sharp as this. Generally it takes more than one speaker to bring the change about; in fact it is usually an event that occurs over an extended period in the anonymous traffic of conversation and letters. Only in a rare case here and there can we actually trace the first speaker, or writer, to have set the process going. But the word "focus" does seem to be just such a case. Kepler appears to have been the first to employ it in its now generally accepted sense as the quasi-center of a geometrical figure—the focus of an ellipse—and it is thought that, in doing so, he had in mind that point in a lens or parabolic mirror, at which the sun's rays are concentrated, so that it becomes a burning glass . . . the burning point, we might say, as the fire in the hearth is a burning point, to gather the warmth and light of the sun (where it all comes from) into the cold and darkness of earth.

A good many years ago the American psychologist J. M. Baldwin remarked that:

> The development of thought . . . is by a method essentially of experimentation, of the use of meanings as worth more than they are as yet recognized to be worth. The individual must use his own thoughts, his established knowledges, his grounded judgments, for the embodiment of his new inventive constructions. He erects his thought, as we say, "schematically" . . . projecting into the world an opinion still peculiar to himself, as if it were true. Thus all discovery proceeds.[1]

And it is really apparent of itself that all radical progress does depend on just this interaction between an individual speaker's meaning and the lexical, or normal, meaning to which Baldwin was pointing when he spoke of what the meaning was "as yet recognized to be worth."

Arthur Koestler, in his book *The Sleepwalkers*[2] (mainly a history of astronomy) went so

1. James Mark Baldwin, *Thought and Things*. London, George Allen & Unwin Ltd., 1911; New York, The Macmillan Company, 1906.

2. Arthur Koestler, *The Sleepwalkers*. London, Hutchinson & Co. (Publishers) Ltd., 1959; New York, The Macmillan Company, 1959.

far as to maintain that, if the analytical rules for the use of language as a means of communication had been strictly enforced in Newton's time, the law of gravity could never have been discovered; or, if discovered, could not have been imparted. This sounds like an amusing exaggeration, and perhaps it is. But let us not be too absolutely sure of it. Newton's law is very familiar and, with the hindsight of familiarity, it is naturally difficult not to feel that there must have been many ways of putting it across without altering the meaning of the word "gravity." Yet progress, that is, radical progress not just hardware improvements—progress involving change—does come about only when we question (and because we question) our fundamental assumptions. Moreover (and this is a crucial point, to which I shall return) the *most* fundamental assumptions of any age are those that are implicit in the meanings of its common words. In our time these happen to be largely the assumptions of nineteenth-century positivism. In Newton's time however they were the assumptions of Aristotelian (that is medieval and premedieval) philosophy, cosmology, and science. In Newton's time an Aristotelian universe was not simply a set of theories, in which men believed—it was what half their key words implicitly *meant*.

Thus, if we really want to put ourselves in their shoes, back at that stage in the history of thought, we must practice thinking, not only about such a thing as gravitation which is easy for us, but rather about something which is correspondingly difficult. Only in that way can we hope to understand their difficulty in thinking about gravitation *at all*. To think of gravity, or of terrestrial physics of any sort, as extending beyond the orbit of the moon was difficult for them *in the same way* that it is difficult for us to think of mind, or mental activity, or intelligence of any sort outside of some particular physical brain. Contrariwise, this (which is so difficult for us) was something that caused them no difficulty at all. It was the sort of thing that the relevant words meant—whereas, for us, the very same words mean the opposite thing—the word "thought" for instance, means, for most people, something rather like cigarettes inside a cigarette box called the brain. One good reason for troubling to concentrate on the moment of change of meaning is that it directs our attention—awakens us—to fundamental assumptions so deeply held that no one even thinks of making them explicit. Try thinking and speaking about "thought" or "thoughts" in the old way, if you want to experience how difficult it must have been, before the scientific revolution, to think about physics in the new way.

So much, then, for expansion of meaning and its dependence on the interaction of speaker's meaning and lexical meaning. But there is also the opposite phenomenon of contraction which we looked at first. In Baldwin's terminology there is also "the use of words as worth [*less*] than they are as yet recognized to be worth." That must also have been brought about by the operation of speaker's meaning on lexical meaning. But there is an important difference here.

Whereas expansion of meaning can be seen to be the product of the mental *activity* of individual speakers, contraction of meaning can also be—it generally is—the product of their passivity. It is more often the product of something like force of habit, or rather the inertia of habit.

Here the parallel discipline that is best able to help us is not history but literature. I mean in particular that part of the study of literature which used to be called, and is still sometimes called, rhetoric. One of the topics with which rhetoric deals is the use of "figurative" language; and a figurative, or metaphorical, use of language is the normal means by which expansion of meaning comes about. It is another name for what happens when a speaker succeeds in making a word mean "more than it is as yet recognized" to mean. Kepler used the word "focus" and Newton used the word "gravity" metaphorically at the time—though they are no longer metaphors *for us*.

Dr. Hugh Blair, who lectured on rhetoric in the eighteenth century, illustrated his remarks on figurative language with a single sentence that happens to contain a number of different examples of it.

> Those persons who gain the hearts of most people, who are chosen as the companions of their softer hours, and their reliefs from anxiety and care, are seldom persons of shining qualities or strong virtues; it is rather the soft green of the soul on which we rest our eyes, that are fatigued with beholding more glaring objects.

If we examine this sentence more closely, we observe, not only that it contains plenty of examples of figurative language, but also that they are examples of different kinds and degrees of figurative language, and I think it becomes apparent on reflection that they are at the same time examples of different proportions in the relation between lexical meaning and speaker's meaning. Thus, in the expression "the soft green of the soul" we ourselves have to do a little imaginative work in order to find ourselves looking through a lexical meaning to a speaker's meaning. For no merely dictionary meaning of the word "green" is normally applicable to the soul. Something the same is perhaps true of the word "shining" in the expression "shining qualities"; and again of "softer" in "softer hours." But, look more closely and you find still other examples—examples this time of expressions which are *in some degree* figurative, but less palpably so. "Those persons who gain the hearts"—could we safely say that the use made here of the verb "gain" or of the noun "hearts" is *not* figurative? To reflect a little even on such a commonplace expression as "strong virtues" is to be reminded that the epithet "strong" has two very different meanings, the one signifying only physical strength, the other properly usable in contexts of quite a different order. Is the second use figurative? Or not?

I spoke just now of "looking through" one sense of a word to another, and I suggest that what is most characteristic of figurative language as a whole is precisely this translucence. Nor do I think that the problem of meaning in general can be usefully tackled without a close look at this phenomenon. But here the historical dimension obtrudes itself on our notice again, whether we like it or not. For instance, I described the figurative expression "strong virtues" as a commonplace one. It is so commonplace that, in this case, the figurative language hardly strikes us as being figurative at all. If we do say that, however, we have let fall a remark whose significance extends far beyond the confines of the art of rhetoric. It takes us, indeed, straight to the kernel of language itself, considered in its historical aspect. Or rather it demonstrates the essentially historical nature of language. It reminds us that, whatever pragmatical advantages may be won by treating language for particular and limited purposes quite unhistorically, its true nature cannot be grasped with exclusion of the time dimension.

Historically observed, the outstanding feature of language in its semantic aspect turns out to be the fact that words which were once figurative have ceased to be so and words that are still figurative are ceasing to be so. Fortunately the later part of the process is one we are able, with the help of some literary taste, to trace even into its finer details. Look for example at the phenomenon of the cliché. During World War I Great Britain was, according to Mr. Lloyd George and the journalists of the day, continually either "in the trough of the wave" or "on the crest" of it (usually, if I remember right, in the trough). "Explore every avenue," "leave no stone unturned," the cliché is a kind of "tired" metaphor, a piece of language on which the passivity of habit (or, as Coleridge called it, "the lethargy of custom") has been at its eroding and contracting work. It has become too commonplace to retain any poetic life as an image, but not common enough to have turned into an inoffensive, recognized "figure of speech." So that you have what has really become a dull lexical meaning (equivalent, in the first instance given, to something like "in great difficulties"), *pretending*, as it were, to retain a spark of speaker's meaning behind it. Whereas in the case of such a recognized figure of speech, as, say, "in dire straits," there is no such pretense. A cliché will in time either be abandoned or it will turn into a "trope," as these recognized figures of speech are sometimes called, and become part of the gear and tackle of reputable discourse.

But even when that has happened, the history of a cliché is not necessarily at an end. It may come to be used so often that it ceases to be even conventionally "figurative"; it may reach a stage where there is no longer *any* translucence, or even pretended or half-remembered translucence, of one concomitant meaning through another; so that what began long ago by being a new and distinguishable "inner," or "immaterial," meaning of a phrase or word will have become its *only* meaning. We have already seen how meanings are contracted by speakers simply dropping part of them altogether.

Emerson was one of those who pointed out that this was the process by which the greater part of our modern vocabulary has been produced. "As the limestone of the continent," he wrote in his essay, "The Poet":

> consists of infinite masses of the shells of animalcules, so language is made up of images, or tropes, which now, in their secondary use,

have long ceased to remind us of their poetic origin.

But Emerson was not alone. It may conceivably be argued that the expression "immaterial meaning" is not a very satisfactory one. It is however not possible to treat of language historically without finding a terminology of some sort for the contrast I am referring to. Material and immaterial—concrete and abstract—physical and mental—outer and inner—we can choose which we like. On the whole I prefer "outer" and "inner," but I have purposely taken the terms "material" and "immaterial" from Jeremy Bentham, because he was one of the founding fathers of a very different view of language from the one I hold myself. He could almost be called a kind of palaeo-logical-positivist, since he also tells us how the immaterial language is erroneously taken by most people to refer to "fictitious entities." Bentham, in his *Essay on Language*, puts it as follows:

Throughout the whole field of language, parallel to the line of what may be termed the material language, and expressed by the same words, runs a line of what may be termed the immaterial language. Not that to every word that has a material import there belongs also an immaterial one; but that to every word that has an immaterial import, there belongs, or at least did belong, a material one.

Whatever else you have in language and its history, then, you certainly have a process by which words with a material, or outer, meaning somehow turn into words with only an immaterial, or inner, one. It has of course been pointed out over and over again that all our words for mental processes—"grasp," "conceive," "understand," etc. can be traced back historically to an earlier stage when they also signified a material process. A very little etymological investigation is enough to reveal that the same thing applies to that whole vast vocabulary of abstractions on which not only the philosophers but the critics, sociologists, politicians, and journalists of today rely so heavily for the purpose of communicating whatever they communicate—"approach," "aspect," "attitude," "condition," "development," "dimension," "dynamic," "expression," "influence," "inhibition," "intention," "integrity" "nostalgia," "opposition," "progressive," "reactionary," "relative," "seminal," "trend," "vision,"—and so on *ad infinitum*.

In all the examples of immaterial language

which I have cited, we are faced with the end product of a completed process. If we want to try and contemplate the process itself and not merely its end product, we must clearly look for instances where it is not yet completed. There is no lack of them. Our excursion into the art of rhetoric merely helped us to examine microscopically a process which is at work in ordinary speech. Take, for example, that group of words which have to do—or (as Bentham might say) "at least did once have to do"—with a man's rank in society, his outward station. In the case of words such as "chivalrous," "courteous," and "gentle," and of course of their opposites, "villainous," "vulgar," etc. we have again mere end products of the process; but we may still notice that in some of the cases its final completion was much more recent than in others. There are circles in England where, for example, the adjective "gentle" (especially in its compounds "gentleman," "gentlewoman") may still be used to denote, or certainly to connote, social position rather than moral quality. In the case of the word "noble," moreover, while the process I have been speaking of is far advanced, it is impossible to say it is completed, though it is nearly so. The concomitant meanings (outer and inner) are still just available. Mostly one uses the word "noble" to signify high moral character and nothing else; but a member of the House of Lords is still referred to in the Chamber as a "noble Lord" without any reference at all to his moral standing. One can quite well imagine a Labour peer remarking in the course of his speech, "We regard the noble lord and his supporters as vermin beneath our notice."

Here there may well be a difference between English and American usage; so that, if it were the latter we were considering, we should have to say that their transition from outer to inner *has* been completed, whereas in England it has not. But even in America I should say that the word "bourgeois" still has exactly the same curious and unfixed concomitance of social and moral senses that I have pointed to in the case of "noble." Perhaps, already, in Russia . . . but, the point is, that you cannot altogether separate meaning from the history of meaning.

In such cases, then, one may observe the process of contraction still actually at work in its various stages. But it is not limited to the domain of sociology, or to any other domain. It has been at work throughout the whole of language. As Bentham reminded us, look far enough back into the history of almost any word of the inner, or immaterial, language, and you come to a period when it had an outer meaning as well. So that its history is, at least in that respect, the story of a contraction of meaning.

It is much less generally realized that the same thing is true of the outer, or material, language. This also is an end product. This also we owe to the process of contraction. Words, which for us today have an outer meaning only, formerly had the inner as well. Moreover, the process by which they have lost their inner meaning is clearly the obverse, or correlative, of the very process by which so many other words have lost their outer meaning.

Both processes may be well illustrated by the histories of such terms as "breath" (or "air" or "wind") and "spirit"; for here they happen to be sharply pointed by a well-known record from a period when they were not as yet completed. In the English version of St. John's Gospel (Chapter 3) we find the following three verses,—in which both terms are employed alternately:

6. That which is born of the flesh is flesh; and that which is born of the spirit is spirit.

7. Marvel not that I said unto thee, Ye must be born again.
8. The wind bloweth where it listeth, and thou hearest the sound thereof, but canst not tell whence it cometh, and whither it goeth: so is everyone that is born of the spirit.

Probably most people read the first part of verse 8 as a metaphor comparing the spirit with the wind. But if we turn to the Greek, we find it is not so. The same word *pneuma* is employed throughout, though it has been (rightly) translated first as "spirit," then as "wind" and then again as "spirit." In Hellenistic Greek *pneuma* still conveyed the concomitant meanings; but the English translators had to split it into two words, one of which ("spirit") had since lost its outer meaning, while the other ("wind") had lost its inner meaning.[3]

In such a word as "heart," on the other hand, (and it is only one of many examples) we

3. The incidence of translation from one language into another, while it happens to illustrate sharply, in no way weakens the point. For the English words "breath," "air," and "wind," or their etymological predecessors, can be shown to have once included the inner meaning no less than *pneuma* did, while "spirit" (Latin *spiritus* meant also both "wind" and "breath") included the outer.

still feel the two meanings concomitant in modern English usage. "Heart" is very commonly used to signify a physical organ conceived as exclusively physical. It is used even more commonly to signify the inner feelings of a man, as is apparent from the adjectives often annexed to it: "warm," "cold," "hard," "soft," etc.

Now the ordinary way of putting it is to say that when we speak of someone having a "warm heart" or a "cold heart," we are using figurative language, using imagery. And that will do well enough, as long as we do not assume that it is the same thing as saying we are using a "metaphor." For the plain truth is that we use the word "heart" as we do, not because we are poets but because the word itself has a history. It is that all language has been, and some still is, imagery, in the sense that one meaning is apprehended transpiring through another. We look back and we find concomitant meanings (or uncontracted meanings that have since become, and are for us now, separable and concomitant); we find an inner meaning transpiring or showing in some way through the outer. Nonfigurative language, on the other hand, is a late arrival. What we call literal meanings, whether inner or outer, are never samples of meaning in its infancy; they are always meanings in their old age—end products of a historical process.

That at least is what we find if we look back into the past as far as the study of language itself will take us. What we may choose to infer about some earlier period or about the origin of speech, on the basis of other studies such as biology or anthropology, is, as we shall see later, another matter.

The words "image" and "imagery" are extremely hard worked just now and are themselves used with a great variety of meanings. I intend, when I use them, that particular sense according to which they signify the transpiring, or translucence, of an inner meaning through an outer, which we have been discussing. This is the sense in which they are largely (though not exclusively) used in the study and criticism of poetry. We are again therefore brought to a point at which the parallel discipline of literature can be of use to us in investigating the nature of language, provided we use it with proper caution. We have, for instance, been hearing a good deal in the last few decades of Mr. Eliot's "objective correlative"—of the poet's search for objects, shapes, patterns, events in the outer world, which can image, in some undefined way, the inner experience he feels impelled to express. When I referred above to "concomitant meanings," I qualified, rather uneasily, by adding "or uncontracted meanings that have since become, and are for us now, separable and concomitant." In doing so, I implied, of course, that you can perhaps also have meanings that are multiple or complex without being separable; and this problem, too, has invited a great deal of attention from those interested in the study or the theory of poetry—those in particular who find in the poet's use of ambivalent, or multivalent, language his chief distinguishing mark as a poet. From both these points of the compass attention is often directed on the use of figurative language in poetry, on the use of simile, metaphor, and symbol.

The three are very much alike but they differ in the degree to which their "soft focus" can, or cannot, be separated by analysis into distinctly focused "meanings." They are all of them forms of utterance characterized by a certain tension between expression and communication; and it would not be difficult to show that it is in metaphor (where the concomitant meanings are less separable than in simile, but more so than in symbol) that that tension is at its highest, though it would take us too far afield to do so. Perhaps for that reason the term "metaphor" is sometimes loosely used to cover all three of them: simile, metaphor, and symbol. Clearly there is a close connection between the poet's use of metaphor (his choice of an objective correlative to express the hitherto unexpressed) and that particular instance of the operation of speaker's on lexical meaning which I classified as *expansion*. Or rather there is more than a close connection. The two are virtually identical. The motivation may be different, the psychological process is the same, when a poet uses a vigorous metaphor to express (as Shelley put it in his *Defence of Poetry*) "the hitherto unapprehended relations of things," or when, in another sphere, Kepler uses the word "focus" in an entirely new way, to embody his own new apprehension. Both of them have to "use words as worth more than they are as yet recognized to be worth." In both cases language is being employed in what I would call, in its widest sense, "the poetic mode."

Now this use of metaphor is fairly common today, especially in poetry. It happens therefore that we are all fairly familiar with this particular species of the genus, "imagery"—this particular species being the expansive operation of an individual speaker's meaning on the lexical meaning of a word or phrase. It is, I believe, for that reason that a certain rash (and in my view, erroneous) conclusion has been drawn by a very large number of people. Thus it is frequently said, and even more frequently assumed without being said, that throughout the whole history of language, and particularly in its early stages, the use of words as metaphors has been responsible, not only for the *expansion* of meaning (as we have been noticing) but also for its contraction. More precisely: what in fact arose by contraction is assumed to have arisen by expansion. We find a word in a dead language, or in a primitive language, that signifies both "wind" or "breath" and "spirit" or "soul"; or we find, in our own time, a word such as "heart"—here are concomitant meanings. How did these words come to have these concomitant meanings in the first place? Oh, because at some remote stage of unrecorded history some individual speaker thought it would be a good thing to use the word "wind" as a metaphor for spirit, or the word "heart" as a metaphor for feeling. Such is the very widespread assumption.

We are all familiar with the use of metaphor in modern sophisticated languages and particularly with the use of it to express the inner experience through the outer "image." And we are also familiar with the way in which metaphors first fade by repeated use and then sometimes fade into actual meanings. So we go on to infer from all this that we know the way in which inner meaning of any sort first found its way into language, and even that we know the way in which inner language arose at all in the first place. We say it arose by way of metaphor.

But that will not do. In order to have a metaphor you must begin by being aware of at least two meanings—two meanings, or sets of meanings, which, however vague and ill-defined they may be in themselves, are not vaguely but sharply distinguished *from one another;* first the lexical, or normal, meaning and, secondly, the speaker's meaning which you now intend the word or phrase "figuratively" to bear. In order therefore to perform the deliberate act of making the outer become a "vehicle" for the inner, you must first have a word with an exclusively outer meaning. But nothing is to be got from the study of language which indicates either that such meanings existed in early times or that they are found today in primitive speech. All that the study of language does indicate is that they have come about as part of that historical process which I have called contraction; whereas the use of metaphor always operates to *expand* meaning. Metaphor cannot therefore have been the original source of what Bentham called the "inner language," though Bentham himself cheerfully assumed that it was. That was why he distinguished so subtly in the second sentence of the passage quoted on page [52]. If he had kept his gaze firmly fixed on the evidence afforded by language itself, he would have written:

To every word that has an immaterial import, there belongs also, or at least did belong, a material one; to every word that has a material import there belongs also, or at least did belong, an immaterial one.

Whereas what he did write was:

Not that to every word that has a material import there belongs also an immaterial one; but that to every word that has an immaterial import, there belongs, or at least did belong, a material one.

In the same way Herbert Spencer, Max Muller, and others in the nineteenth century described with confidence what they called "the metaphorical period" in the prehistoric development of language—a period during which this inner language supposedly made its first entry on the linguistic stage—a period assumed to be already comfortably furnished with a vocabulary that was exclusively "outer" in its reference. There was no warrant for this in the study of language itself; and it must be added that there was no *evidence* for it in any other study. It was all pure speculation.

All the same, this fancy picture of the way in which language developed in its early stages is still endemic, though people no longer speak in express terms of a "metaphorical period." The most one can say is that the number of people who have discarded it is slowly growing. In Cassirer's *Philosophy of Symbolic Forms*,[4] in Bruno Snell's *Discovery of Mind*,[5] in R. B. Onians's *Origins of European Thought*,[6] and elsewhere, not to speak of anthropological stud-

---

4. Ernst Cassirer, *Philosophy of Symbolic Forms*, translated by R. Manheim. New Haven and London, Yale University Press, 1953.

5. Bruno Snell, *Discovery of the Mind*, translated by T. G. Rosenmeyer. Cambridge, Harvard University Press, 1953; New York, Harper Torchbook, 1960.

6. R. B. Onians, *Origins of European Thought*. London, Cambridge University Press, 1951.

ies in the semantics of primitive speech, you will find quite a different picture . . . supported this time by carefully collected linguistic evidence. Even so, the other one remains. In a book called *History and Origin of Language*,[7] which appeared in England about ten years ago, that viewpoint was simply taken for granted; and, from the use he makes of the term "metaphor" to cover all kinds of figurative language at all stages of its growth,[8] it appears to be one of Dr. I. A. Richards's concealed premises that all figurative language originated as metaphor. Yet it is, I have tried to show, only possible to maintain this as long as you have failed to realize that *all* language is, or has been, figurative; for otherwise you would be committing yourself to the statement that language itself originated as metaphor, which is clearly nonsense.

In other words, any such concealed premise must be an illusion. And just as I believe we shall not get very far with the problem of mean-

7. Arthur S. Diamond, *History and Origin of Language*. London, Methuen & Co., Ltd., 1961; New York, Philosophical Society, 1959.
8. I. A. Richards, *The Philosophy of Rhetoric* [New York and London, Oxford University Press, 1930], p. 91.

ing until we approach it historically, so I am
also persuaded that we shall not get very far
with the historical approach itself until we have
got rid of that illusion. I shall therefore return
to it later.

CHAPTER 3

The Psychology of Inspiration
and of Imagination

IT WILL HAVE BECOME APPARENT by now that
the main object of this book is to consider what
light the three subjects of history, language, and
literature can be made to shed on each other.
Now, there is one important respect in which
the third of these subjects differs from either of
the other two. It arises from the fact that poetry, in which literature as a whole had its origin,
and which is still a kind of acronym for literature as a whole, is one of the arts.

Thus, I began by pointing out that, if interest in history as I defined it is itself of comparatively recent origin, consideration of the *theory*
of history is more recent still. The latter part of
this proposition at least will hardly be disputed.
Even if history itself is after all to be deemed as

old as Herodotus, because what the Greeks achieved in the way of history is undoubtedly still important for us, there is nevertheless not much in what the Greeks thought *about* history (if there is anything at all) that remains relevant to our own ideas of it today.

It is much the same with language. Although men were speaking, and men were writing, for millennia before the Greeks were heard of, no really systematic *study* of language was undertaken until a century or two ago.

It is quite otherwise with theory of art. In this case it is not only what the Greeks, for instance, achieved that is still valid; what they thought about it is also still relevant, if only because we can trace fairly easily the stages by which the kind of theory that is held today has developed from the kind of theories they formed. Aesthetic theory is very much older than either theory of history or theory of language. It has a long and significant past of its own.

I shall try in this chapter to take a brief look at that past and see where it leads us. But I find I must begin by drawing attention to an important consideration that affects the history of *any* theory, and indeed the history of ideas in general, no matter what it is that the theories or the ideas are about: namely, that there are two possible causes for people changing their ideas about anything as time goes on. One is that the thing has remained the same, but that the people have come to think differently about it. A mistaken theory, for example, may be replaced by a more correct one; and the reverse is also possible. The other possible cause of a change of ideas is that the thing itself has changed in the meantime. To give a very crude example: looking at them as a whole, our ideas about the economics of transport and commerce have changed enormously in the last hundred years; partly, no doubt, because we have learned to form more efficiently mathematical ideas about anything that is calculable, we have developed the technique of logistics and other aids, but much more because transport itself (and commerce with it) has developed in the meantime from a horse-and-buggy basis to a completely mechanized one. Our ideas and theories have had to change because the thing itself has changed out of all recognition. It is too often forgotten that when it is changing ideas about human consciousness itself we are looking at, or anything so intimately connected with that as artistic activity, the second cause is as likely to have predominated as the first. Ideas have changed because human consciousness itself—the elementary human experience about which the ideas are being formed—the whole relation between man and nature or between conscious man and unconscious man—has itself been in process of change. Indeed I doubt if *"likely* to have predominated" is a strong enough way of putting it. If we think it through, I believe we shall find that it is mainly the second of the two causes we have to deal with here, and that this follows of necessity from the principle that words mean what they are generally used at any time to mean.

In our own time, when people think or write about art or the artist, the word that springs most readily to their minds is "creative." In the expression "the creative artist" the epithet has become almost conventional (like the "learned judge" or the "high-powered executive"). And yet the first thing we find, if we look into the history of aesthetics at all, is that this idea (not just the word, but the idea it expresses) about the nature of art has been formed only very recently. You might say that, although the key word itself was not yet used in the context of art, the idea first began to glimmer through in the seventeenth century. You certainly will not find it any further back. Let us accept the help offered by historical semantics by glancing at a few other such key words and the ideas they express: "genius," for example, which we associate so closely with creativity. In this case the association with aesthetics is much older, so that we can trace, by stages, a gradual development from an older meaning of something like a "tutelary spirit" to its modern meaning. The history of the word "genius" happens to be a case where the semantic approach to history is particularly fruitful, and much the same is true of one or two other words that have become so indispensable a part of the vocabulary of criticism: "original," "imagination," "invention."

The current meanings of all these words have a long and important history. "Genius" will be found to have other etymological associations besides the one I have touched on, including that of sexual potency. For a full treatment of it the reader is again referred to R. B. Onians' *Origins of European Thought,* while the (more recent) histories of the other words in the domain of aesthetic theory were exhaustively considered by Logan Pearsall Smith in the long essay on "Four Romantic Words" in his *Words and Idioms*.[1] Rather than go into details, I want to indicate two particular features in the development of aesthetic theory from its beginning down to our own time, features which are certainly brought out sharply by the semantic approach but which can then be confirmed without having recourse to it.

We normally think of poetry as one of a number of arts; and so, it is clear, did Plato. But, if we now go on to look at the kind of thing Plato said when he was talking about art in general (including poetry but not limiting himself to it) and then at the kind of thing he said when he was talking about poetry only, we find a striking difference. In the first case (thinking of art in general or poetry merely as one among other arts) he treats it as a form of mimesis— imitation. Thus in the *Republic* we are told that poets, and artists in general, are unreliable because they produce imperfect imitations or copies of nature; and Plato adds that, since nature herself is only an imperfect copy of an eternal and immaterial reality, the poet is a man who

1. Logan Pearsall Smith, *Words and Idioms*. London, Constable & Co., Ltd., 1925; Boston, Houghton Mifflin Company, 1926.

supplies us with an imperfect copy of an imperfect copy.

Now one of the things we must certainly do, if we want to trace the past history of the notion we now have of art as a "creative" activity, is to see how this other concept of mimesis changed and developed as time went on—changed, for instance, when the Neoplatonists began insisting that it was not phenomenal nature which the true artist imitated, but the archetypal reality behind nature. So that, according to them, although the artist is an imitator, at least he is not (as Plato himself had feared) an imitator at second remove. In electrician's language the artist stands, not in series with nature, but in parallel with her. This view of the matter remained an influential and persistent one. We find Scaliger, for instance, in the fifteenth century, affirming that "the Poet maketh a new Nature and so maketh himself as it were a new God." Of course he was only using a bold metaphor, especially in the second half of the sentence; but then we have seen that it is through the use of metaphor that meaning expands. We can indeed follow up this particular bit of meaning as it goes on expanding, through the criticism of the

Renaissance—in the doctrines of the Florentine Academy—in the writings of critics like Sir Philip Sidney in England—through the pre-Romantic stir in the eighteenth century and the Romantic ferment in England and Germany in the eighteenth and nineteenth centuries—down to our own time, when the mimetic function attributed to art has, so to speak, been developed away altogether—or transformed—into this new and possibly rather arrogant notion of *creation* as the artist's true function.

The theory of mimesis, then, which is one of the sources of our notion of "creativity," was certainly applied to poetry, and increasingly so as time went on. But it was applied to poetry only as one among the other arts. In fact, in the early stages of the development of the doctrine, the attention of those who were interesting themselves in it was directed more to the visual arts than to the poetic. In particular it was concentrated on the problem of the surpassing excellence of Phidias's colossal statue of Zeus at Olympia, which is no longer extant. Thus, Dio Chrysostom, in the first century A.D., represents Phidias as dealing with the difficulty that "the same image has to be preserved unchanged in the mind of the artist until he has finished the statue, which may be a matter of years." [2] In the following century we have Philostratus speaking of imagination as "an artist who carves what she has not seen." [3] In the next (the third century A.D.) Plotinus is propounding the doctrine that "the arts do not simply imitate what they see but reascend to those principles (*logoi*) from which nature herself is derived . . . Phidias used no visible model for his Zeus." [4] We seem to see the concept of imitation growing before our eyes towards a doctrine of creation.

But in the particular case of poetry (the art whose raw material is language) there was another, parallel, approach to the central aesthetic experience and activity, and it is here we must look for our other source of the psychology of creative imagination.

It has often been remarked that, in spite of his condemnation of poets in the *Republic*, there are other Dialogues (the *Ion* and the *Phaedrus*) in which Plato speaks of the poet with a

2. Dio Chrysostom, Oration XII, *Concerning the Knowledge of God*.

3. Philostratus, *Life of Apollonius of Tyana*, VI, xix.

4. Plotinus, *Ennead*, V, viii.

kind of reverent awe. In these other dialogues
he concerns himself rather with the *psychology*
than with the *method* of poetry. If we really
want to study all that lies behind our current
notion of the creativity of poets and artists, we
have to follow up the history of this line of
thought also and see how it was first developed,
and then finally developed away—transformed.

The poetic psychology, that is, the view of
the psychology of the poet, which was developed in this way, is, of course, the psychology of
inspiration. It is the doctrine of mania, or divine
madness—of *enthousiasmos*—of possession by a
God or by the Muses—and then of possession by
a godling, whom the particular poet refers to as
his Muse; but in any case possession by some
spirit other than the poet's own individual ego.
It was a very persistent psychology. It lived on
(as E. R. Curtius puts it, in his book *European
Literature in the Latin Middle Ages*): [5]

> through the entire millennium which ex-
> tends from the Conquest of Rome by the
> Goths to the Conquest of Constantinople by

5. E. R. Curtius, *European Literature in the Latin
Middle Ages*, translated by Willard R. Trask. New York,
Pantheon Books, Inc., 1952.

the Turks . . . [lived on, until] the creative Eros of the Italian Renaissance reawakened the spirit in the letter.

We must say therefore that the history of poetic psychology is the story of a superindividual psychology, which extends from as far back as can be investigated up to at least the Renaissance, but with reverberations still going on much later; and which only then begins to be transformed into something like an individual psychology. *Then* it becomes, or begins to become, a psychology of individual "genius." And so the word "genius" changes its meaning. Originally the genius was a spirit-being, other than the poet himself (though certainly with a special relation to the poet himself); but that is not what we mean by genius today. The Romans (for it is a Latin word) would never have said of a man that he *is* a genius. They would have said he *had*, or was accompanied or inspired by, a genius. We prefer to say that he is one.

But do not we have to say that, however it may be with muses and genius, we do still take account of something like "inspiration" even today? It is still widely considered that what is operant in the poet or artist in the throes of creation is not quite "himself" in the ordinary, everyday sense. "Something like" inspiration, yes; and that is the whole point. Coleridge, as usual, puts his finger on it, distinguishing implicitly between the old meaning of "genius" and the new, when, in the *Biographia Literaria* he defines true genius as "possessing the spirit, not possessed by it." [6]

To think of Coleridge is, inevitably, to think of the psychology of imagination. Everyone has heard of his distinction between *imagination* and *fancy*, and I need not go into it. But Coleridge serves to remind us that, with the advent of the Romantic Movement (or Romantic Revival, as it is significantly called), with the whole Romantic conception of art, we are passing finally from a psychology of inspiration to a psychology of imagination. Very much has been written about the nature of imagination. It has been pointed out, for instance, that (as the word itself suggests) it has to do with the making of images—images, for example, of nature, which are yet somehow more than mere copies or reproductions.

Perhaps all our endeavors to say something fruitful about imagination can best be seen as a

6. Samuel Taylor Coleridge, *Biographia Literaria*, Ch. 15.

struggle to reject the old concept of inspiration—*and yet somehow retain it*—to reject the old superindividual psychology and at the same time to develop an individual psychology which is viable for the phenomenon of art, and which therefore has to differ sharply from the individual psychology of Hobbes, Locke, and Hume; has indeed to differ from *that* much more sharply than it differs from the older psychology of inspiration. It is felt (or it was until very recently) that both a superindividual and an individual view of the provenance of art are necessary, and must somehow be combined, although they appear to be mutually exclusive. We get, in fact, a kind of polarity of contraries, which is closely analogous to the polarity between *communication* and *expression* that I have suggested underlies the nature of language.

Finally, into all this ferment of aesthetic theory and its development there has entered (almost within living memory) an entirely new leaven in the shape of the concept of an unconscious mind or (as it is sometimes called) the unconscious. I say *almost* within living memory, because this concept of an unconscious mind, though still very young, is nevertheless very much older than Sigmund Freud. We find it, for instance, and in particular relation to the psychology of poetry, in E. S. Dallas's book *The Gay Science*, published in 1866. Dallas has a whole chapter on what he calls "The Hidden Soul"; and he reminds us there that even such a thorough-going Victorian positivist as Herbert Spencer was obliged to postulate this unconscious kind of consciousness; for that is what we really mean when we speak of "the unconscious." Spencer indeed put the matter quite baldly and uncompromisingly when he wrote the sentence Dallas quotes: "Mysterious as seems the consciousness of something which is yet out of consciousness, we are obliged to think it."

The whole pre-Freudian development of the notion of mental activities of which we are unconscious, and which merge with the life forces in us, is usefully traced in Lancelot Whyte's book *The Unconscious Before Freud*.[7]

Broadly, then, this historical transition from a psychology of inspiration to one of imagination is best seen as the transition from a view of art which beholds it as the product of a mind, or

7. Lancelot Law Whyte, *The Unconscious Before Freud*. New York, Basic Books, 1960.

spirit, not possessed by the individual, but rather possessing him; to a view of it as the product of something in a manner possessed by the individual though still not identical with his everyday personality—possessed by him, whether as his genius, or as his shaping spirit of imagination, or his unconscious mind, or whatever name we may prefer to give it. His own, but not himself.

Here the question inevitably arises of the relation between this "superindividual consciousness" and what is commonly, but quite unpicturably, called instinct. Coleridge, for example, in his *Biographia Literia,* speaks of "an interpenetration . . . of spontaneous impulse and voluntary purpose." [8] Earlier in the same work he affirms that only those possess imagination in the deepest sense "who feel in their own spirits the same instinct, which impels the chrysalis of the horned fly to leave room in its *involucrum* for *antennae* yet to come. They know and feel, that the potential works in them, even as the actual works on them!" [9] It would however be a grievous error to equate these "master currents below the surface" [9] with the concept of instinct as it has been developed within the strait jacket of post-Darwinian biological theory. On

8. Coleridge, *Biographia Literaria,* Ch. 18.
9. Coleridge, *Biographia Literaria,* Ch. 12.

the contrary "that which lies *on the other side* of our natural consciousness" [9] is precisely "the spiritual in man." [9] Elsewhere Coleridge himself deals specifically with the whole problem of instinct and, in order to understand what he means, we must first have acquainted ourselves with his general theory of "life." For a similar reason the few remarks I shall venture on the subject myself are best deferred to my final chapter.

There is another difference between the two psychologies we must notice. Whereas the older one (of inspiration) is fundamentally *passive* (as far as an individual mind is concerned), the psychology of imagination is fundamentally *active*. It is normally assumed by us today that the individual poet has to *do* something in order to create poetry. As to exactly *what* he has to do, and with what part of himself, there is little agreement. Not only do theories differ, but the actual experience of one poet differs widely from that of another, if we are to judge by their own accounts of it. Look at the little paperback called *The Creative Process*,[10] in which Brewster Ghiselin has assembled a number of such ac-

10. Brewster Ghiselin, *The Creative Process*, Berkeley, California, University of California Press, 1952. (Mentor series.)

counts. But all seem to agree that he has to do something. Even the extreme view—that all he has to do is to get out of the way, to surrender himself unreservedly to his genius or his imagination or his unconscious or whatever he calls it—comes under this heading. We are left in no doubt that this surrender of the self is a positive act, and even a very difficult one to achieve. What happens is something very different from what happened to Virgil's Cumaean Sibyl, when the divine afflatus descended on her and she shrieked aloud: *Deus, ecce deus!*

If I am right in the suggestion I made at the beginning, that this is a case where the change in theory cannot have been merely a dialectical progress, merely a case of growing accuracy in the observation of the same data, but that it must reflect a change in the data themselves—then we must say that what we have before us, when we look at artistic or poetic activity historically, is an actual transition from one kind of event to another kind. It is a transition from *the being taken hold of by something,* some force or being, or some element of not-self, without any personal effort on the part of the poet, to *an active taking hold of something by* the poet—a producing, an animating, or reanimating of something within himself, which only his personal effort can make available to him. The content of his poetry changes from something that is "given" to something that has to be actively grasped, or achieved.

Does this contrast between a "given" and an "achieved" mental content remind us of anything? Well, it reminds *me* very definitely of that contrast, to which attention was drawn in the first chapter, between the lexical meaning and the speaker's meaning of a word. The lexical meaning (or norm), it will be recalled, is already given in the language which the individual speaker finds available to him. But over against this is the speaker's meaning, which he may or may not produce from himself or achieve somehow in employing that language.

But there is another resemblance also. In both cases, if we look at the matter historically —if we look back *into* the past (which is what we can do with the help of the semantic approach) instead of only looking back *onto* it—and if we do this looking without any preconceived notions derived from other disciplines, then all we can see is the transition from the former to the latter (from the given to the achieved)—or to at least the possibility of achievement. In the case of inspiration and imagination, that transition has been the topic of the present chapter. In the case of language (or rather of meaning), in considering the true nature of imagery and metaphor, we previously observed an over-all *contraction* of lexical meaning leading in to an *expansion* produced by the impact on it of an individual speaker's meaning.

Now, in the case of the history of meaning, attention was further drawn to the fact that historical linguistic theory—that is, etymological theory, and especially the theories characteristic of the nineteenth and early twentieth centuries—has chosen to step outside this fairly simple framework. The theory, for instance, of a "metaphorical period" having occurred at some point in prehistory is the dogma (it is a dogma for semantics, whatever it may be for anthropology or for biology) that these "given" lexical meanings had been produced, or achieved, at a still earlier age in the form of speaker's meaning . . . whereas *the study of language itself* tells us only that speaker's meaning is always *preceded* by lexical meaning.

And so it is with inspiration and imagination. Actual historical study of poetry and of changing ideas about poetry leads us back

through the centuries from a period characterized by imagination to a period characterized by
inspiration. There is nothing in that study itself
that can take us back any further, or to anything
else. But here again, by choosing to import theories drawn from other disciplines altogether
(Comte's positivist interpretation of history for
instance) many, or perhaps most, are led to
assume that the period of inspiration was itself
preceded by a prehistoric ebullience of imagination. The superindividual psychology of inspiration was, we are told (or rather we are not often
told; it is assumed we shall take it for granted),
the invention of a number of anonymous prehistoric individual poets, or philosophers, or scien-
tists, or neurotics. Not only poetry, but also its
predecessor, myth, was, in the first place, the
product not of inspiration, but of imagination.

The concept of myth and the concept of
poetry as the product of inspiration are very
closely allied. And so, lastly, in the theory associated especially with the name of Max Muller,
we find the two dogmas of prehistory, the one
about language and the one about myth, actually coalescing in his definition of myth as a
"disease of language." According to Muller, not
only did the so-called immaterial language—

figurative language—arise in the first place by way of metaphor, but the myths themselves only arose when those metaphors were, by mistake, taken literally. We do not, of course, know who first made that sort of mistake; but we know that a time came when everybody was making it!

Here, then, we have a good example of one of those mysterious mistakes in the use of language which everyone somehow makes at the same time. But, as has already been pointed out, we know better than that today. We know now that language can only mean just what it is employed to mean; so that the idea of a universal mistake *in the use of language* is a nonstarter.

Let us, in conclusion, go back for a moment to history in general, but now also to prehistory. There was Collingwood's dictum that "All real history is history of thought," which is itself based on the sharp distinction he draws between a historical event and a natural one, and so between all history and all nature. It was in this connection that he gave his instance of Caesar crossing the Rubicon. Again without pausing yet to examine the whole of what he says, or to consider how far we can accept it, we must agree, I think, that the distinction between history and nature *is* an important one to make, if we hope to think about either of the two with any degree of precision. The distinction is just as important whether or not, as metaphysicians, we will go on afterwards to resolve it. The existence of anything we can properly call history *does* involve the presence, in or at the back of the relevant events, of some sort of conscious human intention, and therefore of some degree of individual "thought," or of thoughts entertained by an individual mind. Caesar had such individual thoughts when he crossed the Rubicon. It may be that history can take us back to events intentionally brought about by human beings very much less individualized than Caesar, very much less capable of what we now understand by thinking. But *some* degree of it you must have, before you come up to a period in the past which you can talk about at all under the rubric of history. Anything before that would come under the heading of nature. If we liked, we could substitute for the term "historical period" the term "period during which some events were determined by individual thought."

If, for instance, you care to suppose a remote period when sounds were uttered by *Homo sapiens* purely for the purpose of expression and without any supervening element of communication, it would be nature you were talking about—possibly an evolving nature, but still nature, not history. And conversely, as soon as you have individual thinkers, you have reached a period which is properly characterized as "historical" in the wide sense—or, if no records are available, then at least, *pre*historical.

Clearly it was during the prehistoric period that both language and myth developed. Clearly therefore the prehistoric period emerged immediately from something we are only justified in calling nature, just as later the historical period itself emerged immediately from the prehistoric. Yet, here too, the kind of theory I have been engaged in criticizing in the realm of language and aesthetic involves, in the case of history, a sort of leapfrogging movement backwards and forwards at the same time. We are kept on the rails to some extent with the origin of *history,* because there we have the written records to guide us, however much we may misinterpret them. When we come to the origin of *pre*history, then, as far as the psychology of it is concerned, we have mainly speculation. Yet one would have thought that at least we should go on assuming its emergence from nature, and not from the history which only came *after* it.

Nature, as such, involves the *absence*, just as history as such involves the *presence*, of individual human activity, as distinct from "instinctive" behavior. But if we maintain (or, if we imagine or suppose, which is perhaps the commoner failing) that such phenomena as language and myth are *themselves the product* of individual human activity, individual human intention, then we are premising, psychologically, that prehistory emerged, not from nature, but from a still earlier "historical" period—a supposititious period when existentially individualized human beings, not altogether unlike Julius Caesar, thought and imagined and invented and repressed and suffered from neuroses, and did a whole lot of other things which are in fact only possible in—and really only *conceivable* of—the historical period.

CHAPTER 4

Subject and Object
in the History of Meaning

THE AIM of this concluding chapter is to point
to certain far-reaching consequences which flow
from the content of the previous chapters.
There will be no attempt, in the space available, to do much more than point; and it must
be understood that a case is being stated rather
than argued. Since it is consequences I am dealing with, the pointing will itself of course consist
of argument. That is intended to establish not
the case itself (which would require much fuller
treatment), but the fact that there *is* a *prima
facie* case, however disturbing, certainly for further reflection and possibly for further investigation on the reader's part.

It has been shown, then, in the last three
chapters that, if we look back *in*to the past, as

well as looking back *on*to it, we find three things. Looking back in that way at the history of humanity, and even further back into the history of the earth before the physical organism of *Homo sapiens* appeared on it, and particularly if we endeavor to do so with the help of reflection on the nature of language in its historical aspect, we have the following experiences. In the domain of art and poetry we find ourselves looking back through a psychology of imagination into one of inspiration; in the domain of language we find ourselves looking back through what we are accustomed to call literal meaning into figurative or translucent meaning; . . . and lastly we find ourselves looking back through history into prehistory. We find moreover that the period we characterize as prehistory has its own distinctive quality and is not merely history extrapolated. And we find that these three separate perspectives into the past have this in common: that they all involve retrospect through a comparatively recent past, which has been characterized by self-conscious activity—activity of the subject over against the object—into a very much longer preceding one, which was characterized by relative passivity of the subject over against its object.

I am speaking here of "passivity" in the sense that the recipient of anything we can justifiably call inspiration is passive, because he could not be otherwise. If he were otherwise, it would not be inspiration. From this it is necessary to distinguish another kind of mental passivity that concerned us in Chapter 2—the inertia of habit on the part of a subject already existentially freed from its object or, in the case of poetry, "freed" from inspiration. This is the kind that Coleridge called "the lethargy of custom." It is rather bare *inactivity* than passivity strictly understood. But, since both are opposites of activity, there is a risk of the one being confused with the other—a confusion it is vital to avoid.

It has also been emphasized that these perspectives are out of harmony with, or rather directly opposed to, those generally assumed by our contemporaries to be the correct ones. By contrast, our contemporaries assume (for the most part) that—at least in the beginning—something like imagination must be taken to have preceded inspiration; that, in the development of language, literal meaning preceded figurative or translucent meaning; and lastly that an equivalent of history (that is, events involving individual mental activity) came before pre-history. In short, it is assumed that what we may now perhaps call "active subjectivity" preceded the passive subjectivity that was characteristic alike of inspiration, of language in its early stages, and of the prehistoric phase of conciousness.

Here I think is the appropriate place to point out that this tendency to conceive of pre-history in terms of history extrapolated is strikingly exemplified in the historical or evolutionary scheme presented to us by the late Teilhard de Chardin, in his *The Phenomenon of Man* and other books. This is not said to depreciate Chardin. Rather it is because, after all the adverse criticism, I remain impressed by the scope and ingenuity of his thought that I select him as a particularly striking example. Chardin divides his history of the universe into three periods which he designates, respectively, *Matter, Life,* and *Thought.* There is scarcely any reference at all to *language* in *The Phenomenon of Man;* certainly there is no reference at the all-important point where it belongs, which is the point of transition from his second to his third period—from passive life (subjectively passive life) to active thought. Yet, in excluding this, he renounces all possibility of any understanding of the prehistoric phase in the evolution of consciousness.

To return to the perspectives, anyone who puts forward three propositions, and who then goes on to remark that in each case they are almost exactly contrary to the received opinion in his own day, is under a double obligation. In such a case it is not enough for him to argue as faultlessly as he can in support of his own heterodox contentions. He must also (if he is a reasonable man) try to account for the orthodox, and (in his view) erroneous, opinions of the great majority. To take an example, as long as the geocentric view of the solar system continued to be accepted almost everywhere as a matter of course, anyone who preferred the heliocentric perspective was bound not merely to show that it quite obviously gives a much more satisfactory account of the facts as known, but *also* to offer some explanation why, in spite of this, the geocentric perspective should have so long and so universally prevailed.

The first obligation having been discharged to the best of my ability in the preceding chapters, I am now faced with the second. Here I feel myself on dangerous ground, for the reason that most of what I shall be saying is (there is no other word for it) tabu! It probably sounds sensational to put it in that way, but long experience has taught me that it is not. Most people assume that there are no tabus left nowadays in sophisticated society; but they are quite wrong. The old tabus have gone, it is true. Thus, I should feel no embarrassment if the argument obliged me at this point to defend the position of atheism or even of aristocracy in politics, or to advance some new theory of love based on sexual perversion and involving a detailed discussion of the sexual organs in their normal and abnormal manifestation. But the old tabus have merely been replaced by new ones. Those I have just alluded to are dead or dying ones, whereas the one I shall be infringing is very much alive; and a wise man thinks twice before laying sacrilegious hands on the Lord's anointed.

The question is, then: How has it come about that people make the false assumptions they do make before they begin to think at all about imagination, or about the origin and development of language, or about the relation between history and prehistory? It has come about because the whole way in which these subjects are approached, the kinds of questions people are willing to ask themselves or of thoughts they are willing to entertain as even worth examining, are all determined by theories taken over from other disciplines altogether than those of philology or aesthetics or history. The theories, for instance, of biology have been taken over in this way, both directly in the shape of the biological emphasis under which the whole story of evolution is commonly viewed, and indirectly through an anthropology which has itself been based, from the start, on nineteenth-century biological theories of evolution. Unfortunately the whole scope of the ideas regarded as eligible to be entertained concerning the evolution of language and art, and concerning history and prehistory, has been predetermined by results arrived at in disciplines other than their own.

At this point the comment may well be made, Well, what is wrong with that? What could be better? What could be better, or more likely to lead us towards the goal of truth, than that the various disciplines of the human mind—the different sciences—should interact and mutually modify and correct one another?

The answer is that nothing could be better, provided only that all this be done with care and without undue haste; provided, in particular, that neither in our own discipline nor in anyone else's do we make the all-too-common mistake of forgetting to distinguish between actual observation, or actual experience, on the one hand, and hypotheses or theories erected on that observation, or that experience, on the other hand. Otherwise we may find ourselves abandoning a truth which we ought to have retained and accepting an illusion we ought to have detected.

Thus, if someone comes to me, as a historical student of language, and says, "The conclusions you have arrived at concerning the origin and early stages of human speech, which seem to you so inescapable, are incompatible with what I have firmly established in another field of investigation altogether" (or perhaps he puts it more tersely and says, "What you have been saying is very pretty; but of course it is quite unscientific"), then I shall listen to him very carefully indeed. Naturally! Because it may be that I shall have to abandon my inescapable conclusions, go back to the beginning, and set about finding out where I went wrong. But before I go to those lengths I shall want to examine very carefully exactly what it is that my informant *has* established; and, when I have done that, I shall want to use my own judgment, not his, in deciding whether it is in fact incompatible with my own conclusions. This is likely to involve distinguishing rather ruthlessly between the observed facts and the theories erected on them.

In the case of evolution, the observed facts are a variety of surviving vegetable, animal, and human remains, together with the observed results of any chemical or physical analyses to which we can subject them. That and no more. All beyond that is unverifiable, however attractive, hypothesis.

Next, having first been careful to make this all-important distinction, I shall want to examine the theories themselves *as* theories. Can they, for instance, be tested, and have they been tested, by experiment? Here, of course, as in the case of any discipline that seeks to reconstruct *the past* hypothetically, the answer must be no. You cannot predict the behavior of the past and then verify your prediction by experiment. There will be other questions, too, I shall want to ask.

Having assembled all this protective armament round me, I shall then go on to the next step, which is the exercise of my own judgment. For instance, if we pass from the observed facts of the biological and geological panorama to the theories erected on them, we reach first of all the central pillar of evolutionary theory; namely, the idea that in a remote past the vegetable, animal and human kingdoms, whose remains we found preserved in such rich variety, appeared physically on earth in that order—first a vegetable, then an animal, then a human kingdom. I find no difficulty in accepting this hypothesis, verified or unverified, because there is nothing in such an idea incompatible with the observations made in my own field. But of course I do not forget, in accepting it, that what is being spoken of so far is simply the physical forms—the "outside"—of nature. It is the nature we look back *on* to. It is when the next step is taken by the biologists—and it is usually taken in the form of a tacit assumption rather than an explicit deduction—that I find myself compelled, not only to use my own judgment, but actually to prefer my own to theirs. I mean the adoption, together with this chronologically arranged evolution of outsides, of another all-important assumption concerning the evolution of insides, and in particular concerning the inside (or consciousness) of *Homo sapiens*. It is this assumption that colors the popular concept, or no-concept, of "instinct."

The preceding chapters have endeavored to show contraction of meaning as a process that has evidently been characteristic of language from its earliest known stages. Something was also said in them of the counterprocess of an expansion of meaning. Yet, if the presuppositions of the evolutionists are to be accepted, the evolution of consciousness has always been a process of expansion only. The world began (according to them) with nonconsciousness—a kind of existential objectivity without a subject—then consciousness appeared at a point in space located in some physical organism, and then this consciousness progressively expanded, until, in the organism of *Homo sapiens*, it took the form of human consciousness. Thereafter it continued to expand further and further throughout the phases of prehistory and ultimately of history and of modern civilization.

It can be seen that the presuppositions on which this whole picture is based are twofold: a psychological or physiological one, and a historical or chronological one; though it is true that the latter can be resolved into the former, so that in a sense they are one single presupposition. I call them presuppositions now, rather than theories or speculations, partly because they are rarely, if ever, systematically argued and partly because they have been taken for granted by so many for so long that they have gone down into the unconscious and become implicit in the meanings of all sorts of words we habitually employ to think with.

To pause here and give one or two examples: there is the adjective "collective" in Jung's concept of a "*collective* unconscious." The term "collective" already implies an aggregation of pre-existing self-contained units, and therefore presupposes that an expansion from individual to group experience preceded any contraction from group to individual. Again, there is the word "animism," when used by anthropologists or in any discourse on the nature and origin of myths. This "fixes" a certain presumed original relation between man and nature in much the same way that "collective" fixes a presumed original relation between individual and group consciousness. And here I find it worth remarking that the poet C. Day Lewis in his book *The Poetic Image*[1] uses this word very differently,

1. C. Day Lewis, *The Poetic Image*. London, Jonathan Cape, Ltd., 1947; New York, Oxford, University Press, 1947.

and less misleadingly, when he affirms (in speaking of the images used *in modern poetry* and thus of an expansion of consciousness) that "every image is animistic." In philosophy, I trace the presuppositions in the meanings of such words as "empirical" and "transcendental." But of course it is not only a matter of such semitechnical terms as I have just now instanced. There are the everyday words like "reality." Although the matter of this chapter was described at its outset as "far-reaching," it is also incisively significant in many intimate and ostensibly circumscribed contexts. Literary criticism is one of these; as anyone may verify for himself, who will take the trouble to abstract the presuppositions given in, for example, Professor F. R. Leavis's repeated applications of "real," "reality," "realize," "concrete" in arriving at his value judgments.[2]

The first of the two presuppositions is that "inwardness," subjectivity of any sort, is not merely *associated with,* but is always the *product of* a stimulated organism. The second, aris-

2. Compare with Vincent Buckley, *Poetry and Morality* [London, Chatto and Windus, Ltd., 1961; New York, Humanities Press, 1959] Chapters vi and vii (particularly p. 208).

ing out of it, is the presupposition that in the history of the universe the presence of what is called "matter" preceded the presence of what is called "mind." To these two one could perhaps add a third, namely, that the "public" world (which is what we have in common with others) consists entirely of what we *perceive* and the private world of each one consists of what he *thinks*. For the reasons given at the beginning of the chapter, I must dispose of this third one in a parenthesis. It is not very difficult to show that, on a strictly distributive analysis of the complex blend of thought and perceptions which constitutes what we normally experience as outside of and other than ourselves, the exact opposite is the case. It is the thought content which we share with others, while our percepts (so far as they are undetermined by *any* element of thought) are private to ourselves. It would be fairly easy to show this, but not without a considerable digression.

It is perhaps now becoming apparent why I began by calling these two presuppositions "tabus." When presuppositions get into the lexical meanings of words and thus into the unconscious itself, they are apt to become tabus in the sense that, when people start thinking about some topic or other, the near prospect that their train of reasoning may be leading to a conclusion which will infringe the tabu causes them to stop reasoning and make a jump of some sort. This is particularly apparent in our own day, when near prospects of just that kind of conclusion are beginning to open up in a good many fields of inquiry. As examples of these I shall adduce the increasing prominence of so-called "holistic" theories in biology, psychology, and philosophy; the concept of Gestalt in psychology; and, in general, an increasing realization of the causal significance of "pattern" (as distinct from "particle" or "impact"). In physics, moreover, there is the discovery of the implication, already at the nuclear level, of the observer in what he observes. Nor would I omit the endeavor, already noticed in Chapter 1, to set up history as no longer merely a branch of natural science, but as a separate mode of knowledge altogether.

Now all these lines of thought (if they are followed through to the end) may lead to conclusions infringing the tabu. They are therefore not followed through to their logical conclusion, but at a certain point in the reasoning fantastic leaps are made (that old hypothesis of a "metaphorical period" for instance), so as to enable them to be hustled into accord with the prevailing climate of opinion—with the tabus, in fact. We have already reminded ourselves where the general body of modern *knowledge* stands concerning the actual relation of natural object to thinking-perceiving subject. One great advantage of reading the history of language as it stands before us, unbowdlerized by the tabus, is the making unnecessary these reluctant intellectual contortions on the brink of the chasm between what everybody really *knows* and what everyone feels positive about.

I shall refer once again to R. G. Collingwood's *Idea of History,* because one part of it affords a particularly striking example of what I mean. In my first chapter I cited his principle that "all real history is history of thought"; and the reader was reminded how, in support of this, he points out that, when the same thought occurs in two different minds, you have not two separate thoughts (the one being a detached replica of the other), but "one and the same thought." You have, as emphasized by Collingwood himself, not merely identity but numerical identity. At this point I remarked that this was the kind of statement that made people feel uneasy; and I did so because this observation on the nature of thought is in flat contradiction of the presupposition that thought is the product of a stimulated physical organism. If taken seriously, it transgresses the first tabu.

If a concept in my mind is one and the same with the concept in yours, then it clearly cannot be the product of either my organism or yours. It cannot be dependent on those organisms any more than the light we both see by is dependent on your eye or mine. It is not light that is dependent on an eye, but the experience of seeing. However, the point I want to make is that, because it is tabu, Collingwood makes it clear, as he proceeds, that, although he *says* this about thought, he does not really believe it! Although he has propounded it himself, and propounded it cogently and precisely, he finds he cannot believe it. It would be too great a deviation. And so, like all the others, he side-steps, rather than pursue his own train of reasoning whither it must inevitably lead him.

For if he had really believed what he said, he of all men could never have gone on to draw the kind of distinction he does draw between man and nature—that distinction on which he has based his whole doctrine of the unbridgable gulf between history and science. He bases that doctrine on the presupposition, which he takes for granted, that man has what he calls an "inside," but nature has no "inside." Thought, of which he says history consists, is the inside of man and his actions. But nature has no corresponding inside—no inside at all. We see that, in denying an inside to nature, he is really still conceiving thought as the product of man's physical organism, although this is quite incompatible with that view of the superindividual essence of thought which he himself has just categorically stated.

Possibly I have now succeeded in making clear why I select such a sensational term as tabu. I am not of course saying that there is any embargo on a man's arriving at, and even expounding, some kind of idealist philosophy or other, some abstract theory or rational demonstration that mind must be conceived as anterior to matter—Berkeleyism, Kantianism, neo-Kantianism, Bergsonism, Buddhism—there is a wide choice. No. What the tabu enjoins is that he shall put all that out of his mind as soon as he lays down his pen or leaves the lecture room; above all, that he shall not attempt to apply it in any other realm of inquiry that he may enter, an inquiry for instance into the origin of language, or of myth, or (if he happens to be a scientist) into the basis of post-Cartesian scientific method. As soon as he goes on to do this, he is bound as a respectable member of educated society to start off from a whole array of presuppositions that are quite incompatible with the conclusions he has arrived at as philosopher or physicist or whatever.

It was indicated in the course of the first three chapters that at least in my own field of study everything points to an evolution of consciousness, which, up to as recently as three or four centuries ago, has mainly taken the form of a contraction of meaning and therefore of consciousness—an evolution from wide and vague to narrow and precise, and from what was peripherally based to what is centrally based. Further, that if this predominance of contraction is demonstrably true of the historical period up to now, it was even truer of the prehistoric period. If history has been par excellence the period of developing thought, prehistory was par excellence the period of developing language—the period of the original emergence of speaker's meaning from lexical meaning, the period therefore during which man was slowly and painfully extracting his subjectivity from language; that is, as Cassirer, for one, has so convincingly demonstrated, from the inside of nature through the medium of language. It must be admitted that this is a topic on which it is difficult to be concise without being inaccurate. "Man was extracting . . . ," it was said, but since the very thing he was extracting was his subjectivity, he ought not to have been made the subject of a sentence at all. "The period during which man's subjectivity was being extracted . . ." would have been more accurate, if less elegant.

Finally, I have tried in this chapter to suggest that our backward glance cannot really stop at prehistory. We are inevitably taken back, behind the prehistorical, to what is perhaps best called the "primeval" period; or, in other words, to nature herself. It was at this point that Collingwood executed his side step; and he no doubt did so because the "nature" to which we are thus led back must be so very different from the primeval nature assumed by the evolutionists. We cannot help that. We are no longer in the shoes of Collingwood and his contemporaries. Once we have smashed the first tabu— once we have transferred the shadowy and forbidding figure with outstretched arms from the twilight of its native grove, in which we have hitherto been beholding it, to the dry light of the museum where it belongs; and have seen that, after all, it is only a carved wooden totem pole—we are through, not only with the first tabu, but with the second also.

As a result, we find ourselves with a nature very different from the nature assumed by the evolutionists. But the odd thing is that, once one has got over the shock, this nature turns out to be *more*, not less, like the nature we actually see, hear, and smell and generally experience around us—easier, not harder, to believe in than theirs!

The plain fact is that if we really *look* at nature—if we really observe her without the tabu at the back of our minds—there is nothing whatever to suggest that she has "no inside." Indeed, there is everything to suggest the contrary. The concept of "instinct," however it is taken, alone implies as much. For instinct cannot be understood, cannot honestly be conceived, otherwise than as a superindividual wisdom at work in nature. This is again a matter which could not now be pursued without our being carried too far afield. However, if anyone is minded to examine the relation between instinct and wisdom, and again between both of these and what we call the "unconscious" in man, I would recommend him to consult some of E. L. Grant Watson's books, and particularly perhaps the one that appeared in 1964 under the title of *The Mystery of Physical Life*.[3]

We are free at last, then, if there is anything at all in what has been said, to accept what the whole character and history of language cries aloud to us: namely, that the prevailing assumption that matter preceded mind in the history of the universe is a historical fallacy, and, alas, one with far-reaching consequences. It becomes clear to us that, both ontogenetically and phylogenetically, subjectivity is never something that was developed out of nothing at some point in space, but is a form of consciousness that has *contracted* from the periphery into individual centers. Phylogenetically, it becomes clear to us that the task of *Homo sapiens*, when he first appeared as a physical form on earth, was not to evolve a faculty of thought somehow out of nothing, but

3. E. L. Grant Watson, *The Mystery of Physical Life*. London and New York, Abelard-Schuman Limited, 1964.

to transform the unfree wisdom, which he experienced through his organism as given meaning, into the free subjectivity that is correlative only to *active* thought, to the individual activity of thinking.

As the history of philosophy reflects the latest stage of this agelong process, so the semantic history of the words "subject" and "subjective" reflects the history of philosophy. Thus, for "subjective," we find in the Oxford English Dictionary, supported by quotations, the lexical meaning, in the seventeenth century: *pertaining to the essence or reality of a thing; real, essential.* A further lexical meaning, but dating back now only to the first half of the eighteenth century, is: *having its source in the mind.* By the second half of the same century we have: *pertaining or peculiar to an individual subject or his mental operations . . . personal, individual.*

So far, we have the connotation of reality plus a steadily increasing emphasis on the activity of the individual. It is reserved for the second half of the nineteenth century to go to the length of actually reversing the meaning in one respect, so that the adjective whose lexical meaning was *real, essential,* becomes an adjective whose lexical meaning is: *existing in the mind only, without anything real to correspond with it; illusory, fanciful.*

It is clear, I think, that this equation of individualized mind with unreality, which is implicit in its predominant lexical meaning today, irrupted into *subjective* from the factitious picture, prevalent in the nineteenth century, of a world of existential objects chronologically anterior to any existential subject (and therefore supposed more "real")—a world of outsides with no inside to them. We have forgotten that the concept of an object without a subject is as abstract as the concept of a surface without a depth and as futile as that of a back without a front.

As against this, I have contended that an over-all historical semantic points to successive phases marking a progression from one type of subject-object relation towards another; from the state of active object, correlative to passive subject, to the state of passive object, correlative to active subject.

Moreover, since the two *are*, and must always have been, correlative, a change in the relation between them is at the same time a radical alteration in both of the principles themselves. It is this unfixedness of both object and subject, as I have already indicated in the first chapter, that constitutes the fatal weakness of behaviorism as a philosophical or scientific system, whatever value it may have, either for psychology or for linguistics, as an *ad hoc* technique adopted for certain limited purposes.

But it is also the fatal weakness of antihistoricism. For antihistoricism is based on an unargued presupposition that the relation between subjective man and an objective world, which he experiences and with which he has to deal, has always remained fundamentally the same. In one period he has dealt with it in one way, in another period in another—rather as a sick man turns first onto this side and then onto that, hoping to find the most comfortable accommodation for his aching limbs. The late H. A. L. Fisher put the case for antihistoricism incisively as well as ironically in the preface to his *History of Europe*:

> Men wiser and more learned than I have discerned in history a plot, a rhythm, a predetermined pattern. These harmonies are concealed from me. I can see only one emergency following upon another as wave follows upon wave, only one great fact with respect to which, since it is unique, there can

be no generalizations, only one safe rule for the historian: that he should recognize in the development of human destinies the play of the contingent and the unforeseen.[4]

The picture has some truth in it, but it is not the whole story. Harmonies will always remain "concealed" from those who decline to look in the only direction where they could possibly be found; as the harmonies from a piano are not to be found by confining our attention to the unforeseen and eccentric behavior patterns of its keys.

If nature has no inside, then neither has history; for the "thought," which Collingwood cast for that role,[5] can be no more than a flicker in the skulls of a string of creatures whose lives are nasty, brutish, and short. But the historical study of language does point us to an "inside" of both man and nature and, in doing so, reveals a clear enough "plot" extending from nature through prehistory into history. As to the "rhythms," I do not see why an intelligent person should even start looking for any until he

4. Herbert A. L. Fisher, *History of Europe*. 3 vols. London, Edward Arnold & Co., 1936; Boston, Houghton Mifflin Company, 1935–1936.

5. See Chapter 1, page 21.

has first conceded that there *is* a plot—that it is a play we are watching and not just a romp or a harlequinade. And my suggestion has been that, just as it is with an ordinary play, we can only make that discovery by not merely watching happenings but also understanding words.

Index

Activity, mental: 46,
    83–91, 93–95, 114–
    15
Aesthetic theory: its his-
    tory, 69–91
"Animism," 103–5
Antihistoricism, 17,
    116–17
Aristotle, 24–25
Artist, creative: history
    of the term, 71–91
Auerbach, Erich, 14

Bacon, Francis, 14
Baldwin, J. M., 43, 46
Barfield, Owen, 25
Bentham, Jeremy, 52–
    56, 64
Berkeley, George, 32
Biographia Literaria
    (Coleridge), 79, 82

Blair, Hugh, 47
Buckley, Vincent, 104
Bury, J. B., 16

Caesar, Julius, 21, 23,
    88–89, 91
Cartesian Linguistics
    (Chomsky), 38
Cassirer, Ernst, 65, 111
Chardin, Pierre
    Teilhard de, 95–96
Chomsky, Noam, 38
Chrysostom, Dio, 75
Cliché, 50–51
Coleridge, S. T., 14, 39,
    50, 79, 82–83
"Collective uncon-
    scious," 103–5
Collingwood, R. G., his
    view of history, 17–
    23, 88, 107–9, 111, 117

Communication, 28–30, 35–39. *See also* Language

Comte, Auguste, 87

Consciousness: author's views about development of, 102, 110–15. *See also* Unconscious; Subjectivity

Contraction (of a word's meaning), 32–33, 40, 46–59, 62–67, 102, 110–15

Contraries, polar. *See* Polar contraries

Creative artist: history of the term, 71–91

Creative Process, The (Ghiselin), 83

Curtius, E. R., 77–78

Dallas, E. S., 81

Day Lewis, C., 103–4

Defence of Poetry (Shelley), 61

Diamond, Arthur S., 66

Discovery of Mind (Snell), 65

Eliot, T. S., 59

Emerson, Ralph W., 51–52

Essay on Language (Bentham), 52–53

European Literature in the Latin Middle Ages (Curtius), 77–78

Expansion (of a word's meaning), 32–33, 39, 41–46, 59–63, 74, 102

Expression: as a function of language, 35–39

Figurative language: historical importance of, 46–67, 93–95

Fisher, H. A. L., 116–17

"Focus," 41–42, 47, 61

Ford, Henry, 17

Freud, Sigmund, 81

"Furniture," 31–32, 40

Gay Science, The (Dallas), 81

"Genius": changing notions about, 72–73, 78–85

Ghiselin, Brewster, 83

Gospel according to St. John, 56–57

Grant Watson, E. L., 113

"Gravity," 41, 44–45, 47

"Heart," 57–58

Herodotus, 13, 69

History: defined, 13;

changes in perceptions of, 13–23; words dealing with, 14–15; as a method of cognition, 19–23; causes of false assumptions about, 97–110; its relation to nature, 88–91, 117–18; its relation to science, 108–9. *See also* Prehistory; Primeval period; Semantic approach to history

History and Origin of Language (Diamond), 66

History in English Words (Barfield), 25

History of Europe (Fisher), 116–17

Hobbes, Thomas, 80

Hume, David, 80

Idea of History, The (Collingwood), 17, 107–9

Idea of Progress, The (Bury), 16

Ideas: causes of changes in, 70–71

Imagery: defined, 59. *See also* Figurative language

Imagination: psychology of, 79–91, 93–95; causes of false assumptions about, 97–110

Immaterial. *See* Material *vs.* immaterial

Inspiration: psychology of, 77–91, 93–95

Instinct: concept of, 82–91, 102, 112–14

Ion, The (Plato), 76

John, Gospel according to St., 56–57

Jung, Carl G., 103

Kepler, Johannes, 41–42, 47, 61

Koestler, Arthur, 43

Language: functions of, 35–39; causes of false assumptions about origins of, 97–110. *See also* Figurative language; Thought; Words

Leavis, F. R., 104

Lewis, C. Day, 103–4

Lewis, C. S., 27, 31–32, 34

Lexical meanings (of

words), 27–39, 42–67, 85–86, 105–7, 110

Literal meanings: as end products of historical process, 58–59, 93–95

Lloyd George, David, 50

Locke, John, 80

Material vs. immaterial, 52–67, 105, 113

Mathematics, 36

Matter. *See* Material *vs.* immaterial

Meaning. *See* Contraction; Expansion; Figurative language; Lexical meaning; Literal meaning; Speaker's meaning; Words: changes in meaning of

Mental activity. *See* Activity, mental

Mental passivity. *See* Passivity, mental

Metaphor, 60–67, 74–75

"Metaphorical period," 64–67, 86, 107

Mimesis. *See* Aesthetic theory: its history

Mimesis (Auerbach), 14

Mind. *See* Material *vs.* immaterial; Subjectivity; Thought

Misuse of words, 29–30

Muller, Max, 64, 87–88

Mystery of Physical Life, The (Grant Watson), 113

Myth, 87–91, 103

"Natural," 33–34

Natural science: its relation to history, 18–21, 108–9. *See also* Nature

Nature: its relation to history, 88–91, 117–18; Collingwood's views of, 108–9; author's views about, 110–12. *See also* Natural Science; Primeval period

Neoplatonists, 74

Newton, Isaac, 41, 44, 47

"Objective correlative," 59–61

Onians, R. B., 65, 72

Origins of European Thought (Onians), 65, 72

Paradox, 38

Passivity, mental, 46, 83–91, 93–95

Past, the: changes in perceptions of, 13–23. *See also* History; Prehistory; Primeval period

Phaedrus, The (Plato), 76

Phenomenon of Man, The (Teilhard de Chardin), 95–96

Phidias, 75–76

Philosophy of Rhetoric (Richards), 66

Philosophy of Symbolic Forms (Cassirer), 65

Philostratus, 76

Plato, 24, 73–77

Plotinus, 76

"Pneuma," 57

"Poet, The" (Emerson), 51–52

Poetic Image, The (Day Lewis), 103–4

Poetry: history of. *See* Aesthetic theory: its history

Poetry and Morality (Buckley), 104

Polar contraries, 38, 80

Prehistory: author's views about, 88–91, 93–96, 102, 110; causes of false assumptions about, 97–110; its connection with history, 117. *See also* Primeval period

Primeval period, 111

Republic, The (Plato), 73

Richards, I. A., 66

Scaliger, J. C., 74

Science, natural. *See* Natural science

Semantic approach to history, 25–26, 30–35, 44–67, 117–18

Shakespeare, William, 14

Shelly, P. B., 61

Sidney, Philip, 75

Simile, 60–61

Sleepwalkers, The (Koestler), 43–44

Smith, Logan Pearsall, 14–15, 72–73

Snell, Bruno, 65

Speaker's meaning (of words), 27–39, 42–67, 85–86, 110

Spencer, Herbert, 64, 81

Spengler, Oswald, 16

Studies in Words (Lewis), 27, 31–32, 34

"Subjective," 33, 114–15

Subjectivity, 95, 104–5, 111, 113–15

Symbol, 60–61

Tacitus, 13

Teilhard de Chardin, Pierre, 95–96

Thought: relation of words to development of, 43–67; its relation to historical periods, 88–91; Collingwood's views on, 107–9

Thought and Things (Baldwin), 43

Thucydides, 13

Toynbee, Arnold J., 16–17

Translucence (of figurative language), 49–51, 59, 93–95

Trope, 51

Unconscious: origin of concept of the, 80–91; collective, 103–5. *See also* Consciousness; Subjectivity; Thought

Unconscious Before Freud, The (Whyte), 81

Vico, G. B., 16

Virgil, 84

Vocabulary, historical, 14–15

Watson, E. L. Grant, 113

Whyte, Lancelot, 81

Words: their relation to the past, 23–39, 44–67, 116–17; wrong use of, 29–30; changes in meaning of, 40–67; their material and immaterial meanings, 52–67. *See also* Lexical meaning; Literal meaning; Semantic approach to history; Speaker's meaning; Thought

Words and Idioms (Smith), 73

About the Author

OWEN BARFIELD, at ninety-one, is a solicitor and philosopher whose books have won respect on both sides of the Atlantic from many writers, including Tolkein, Eliot, and C. S. Lewis. He was born in North London in 1898 and received his B.A. with first-class honors from Wadham College, Oxford, in 1921. He also earned B.C.L., M.A., and B.Litt. degrees from Oxford and is a fellow of the Royal Society of Literature. He served as a solicitor for twenty-eight years until his retirement from legal practice in 1959. Barfield has been a visiting professor at Brandeis and Drew Universities, Hamilton College, the University of Missouri at Columbia, UCLA, SUNY-Stony Brook, and the University of British Columbia, Vancouver. His books include nine others published by Wesleyan: *Poetic Diction*, *Romanticism Comes of Age*, *Saving the Appearances*, *Worlds Apart*, *Unancestral Voice*, *What Coleridge Thought*, *The Rediscovery of Meaning*, *History, Guilt, and Habit*, and *Owen Barfield on C. S. Lewis*. His home is in East Sussex, England.